WILDER

A SOCIAL JUSTICE
PHANTASY

Incorporating ideas of Rawls, Sartre, Kant, and Marx

BOB BOGNER

outskirts
press

Table of Contents

Preface

The purpose of this short book is to present, in an easy to understand form, the basic concepts contained in John Rawls' book, "Justice as Fairness," (Rawls, 2001). If the reader is enlightened by "Wilder," I encourage s/he to read Mr. Rawls' book for a much more detailed description of the ideas "Wilder" presented.

Introduction

"Wilder"

George and Karen are going to have a baby! It will be born into their society, with their genes and DNA…a simple concept to understand. Looking at the same situation from the perspective of the baby is much more complicated.

The baby to be born, who we shall call Wilder; what of Wilder? Wilder's soul is placed in the embryo that George and Karen created; but why is this particular soul put into this particular child, with these particular traits, at this particular time, to be born in this particular society? Why wasn't Wilder's soul placed with a child born during the Crusades, the renaissance, or even prehistory? Why was Wilder born to George and Karen, with their genes and DNA, rather than to Isadore and Racheal, Riki and Alan, or Max and Esther? Why weren't you or I born as Wilder? Does a super-natural force decide these events, or are they determined by chance? I spend much time contemplating this question, but as for answering it, I cannot. Illustrating this perplexity itself is an aspect of my writing; but it is the questions that the illustration leads to that are the crux of the pages that follow.

For the sake of what follows (and only for that sake as I do not have the answer as to how the traits and society a soul is given are determined), Wilder's traits and society will be determined by a "creator" because the basic subject of this prose, justice, can be presented in a clearer manner then by referring to a "creator" than if "chance" or "God" is used as the determining factor.

Wilder is a fictitious "soul" who has lived many different lives; He/she is a thinking fetus with no determined traits and no knowledge of what type of society or what situation within that society he/she will be placed. Wilder is a soul with the ability to think and communicate with other souls. This may be difficult to comprehend, but it is necessary for the thought experiment we will be immersed in.

Since Wilder cannot be described as either male or female in pre-birth situations, the designation I will use for pronouns (he/she, his/her, etc.) referring to Wilder and his/her friends in situations where Wilder's sex has not been determined is ❓. The reader may substitute any pronoun for ❓ to make the sentence more readable. My intention is to encourage the reader to think and realize that Wilder is not provided with any natural traits before birth. Once Wilder or his/her friends is "dropped-into" a society, traits and gender are established, and normal personal pronouns are used. The word [c] Creator is used with either a lower case or capital letter to indicate the force, whether it be God, nature, or chance, that is responsible for one's inborn traits and drop-in society.

BOOK I

CHAPTER 1

Thought Experiment (Part One)

"WILDER"

In order to keep the reader's focus on Wilder's situation as a pre-born human being with no attributes such as height, eye color, race, or sex; "Wilder," and Wilder's friends will be referred to in situations in which he/she is pre-birth as ❓. If at first the reader finds this confusing, he/she should substitute the name "Wilder", or an appropriate pronoun in place of ❓.
Because some people believe in a Holy Deity and some don't, the "C(c)reator" will be randomly spelled with a large or small case letter.

On Being Born

Wilder is nervous, today is the day ❓ will appear before the "Creator" to begin the process of determining ❓ inborn traits and the society that ❓ will be "dropped-into." Wilder does not know what ❓ next life will be, but soon, at the interviews, ❓ will find out. The creator, by first establishing the traits Wilder will be born with and then inserting ❓ into a society— will determine the parameters of the next life ❓ will lead. Wilder is a soul, and in Wilder's universe (as in the Hindu religion) a soul never dies, but is reborn time after time; however, unlike the Hindus, Wilder is conscious between deaths and re-births.

Imagine yourself in Wilder's position: a soul waiting for a body… a soul waiting to be born … at this moment without sex, without age, without any physical or mental attributes (height, sensory capabilities, intelligence, etc.). What traits will Wilder's body be endowed with, what type of society will Wilder be inserted into; will Wilder be 6' 6" tall, 4'8" small, or somewhere between; black skinned, brown skinned, yellow, or white; male or female… will Wilder be physically/mentally challenged or healthy? Wilder has no idea! Wilder wants to be attached to a healthy body; but if ❓ body is sickly, how will the society that Wilder is dropped into treat Wilder: will it take care of ❓, or will it ignore or discard ❓? What are Wilder's chances of being inserted into a wealthy society, compared to a poor one; of being in the upper socio/economic strata of the society ❓ is dropped in, compared to being dropped into the lower strata; of being born into a single parent situation, gay family, or a "normal" family situation? All these possibilities are swirling through Wilder's mind. Imagine!

How would you feel before meeting your "Creator?" What would you hope for? Or, if you could bargain, what would you settle for? Some of Wilder's previous lives were so horrendous ❓ certainly wouldn't want to do them over. Wilder would prefer not to be born rather than live the life of a colonial slave again, but Wilder has no choice as to whether to be born or not…like us, Wilder will be born, the question facing Wilder is not whether to be born, but under what conditions will ❓ be born?

At this point in time, since none of the souls/beings have been granted their inborn traits or their social position…they are all equal. They are in what we will call "the original position," (Rawls, 2001). This will change after the creation interviews when they will not be equal any longer due to the distribution of their inborn traits and their newly established places in society. It is at this point of time, when all beings are equal, that our thought experiment begins: it revolves around justice and fairness.

The Creation Interview

The first step in Wilder's ordeal is the "creation" interview. During this interview, the Creator informs Wilder of the natural attributes of the body and mind that Wilder's soul will inhabit. Inborn traits influence a being's life, they set parameters on what a person can do.

For example:

Imagine that your goal in life is to be a professional basketball player. You love the game — you practice every spare moment of your time. Your parents and coach tell you, "follow your dream, work hard and the results will come," but the creator decided you were going to be 5'4" tall. Do you think you could realize your dream? I doubt it, since the inborn trait of height is so important to a basketball player. Or, once again, using the basketball analogy; this time you are 6'4" tall, and again you practice every spare moment, and the practice enables you to compete at the high school level of play; but your friend, who is only 6'2" tall and plays football and baseball also (thus not able to practice basketball as much as you do) makes it to the college level in all three sports...and he didn't even care about basketball that much, he chose to be a professional baseball player. Why: The Creator endowed him with superior athletic traits, he was lucky, at least in this aspect of his life.

The same scenario appears in many other aspects of life: music, intellectual endeavors, art, business, and most importantly, health. The point is that after the first meeting with the creator, *all beings are no longer equal.* Some are endowed with traits that will make it easier for them to succeed in their goals, while others, who may try much harder will not. Is this fair, no; is it true, absolutely. The following are some of the inborn traits to be decided at the first interview...the creation interview.

Skin color and race. It is well documented in many societies that the inborn trait, race and/or the color of one's skin, affects one's ability to have a job, be treated fairly before the law, vote, obtain an education, and be treated with dignity. Wilder, having lived previous lives including some of which ❓ has been racially oppressed, feels that this is a strange social phenomenon, as Wilder is the same soul regardless of what color pigment the whim of the creator bestows on ❓ skin. The trait of race/skin color is innate, but prejudice due to skin color is not innate, it is learned. That does not make it any less of a fact, nor any less hurtful. Uneasiness concerning the "race issue" builds inside Wilder. Will ❓ life's ambitions be limited because of ❓ race, or will ❓ have an expanded perspective on life's rewards because ❓ is "lucky enough" to be born "white" or inserted into a society with little racial bias?

Sex. Females bear children, which automatically differentiates the roles of male and female; but being a woman rather than a man means more than that. Until the 20th century, women in most societies composed a subset of humanity significantly inferior to men: men were the heads of households in which women were considered property, women did not have the right to vote, could not serve in the military, and if permitted to hold a job outside of the home, were not paid on the same scale as men. Things have changed somewhat, but there is still prejudice against women in the 21st century, mostly related to job force and abortion issues. Aside from job related inequalities, women must directly confront "right to life" and "choice" issues. As a woman in the US, a state may restrict your choice of control of your own body; men may be concerned with these women's issues, but not in the same direct manner that women are.

Women being treated as inferior to men is not true in all societies; other societies, past, present, and future, treat the sexes differently: some societies are matriarchal (women having more power than men), some patriarchal (men having more power), and some treat males and females equally; but whatever society a being is born into, the outlook is different if you are born a man, or born a woman.

Wilder is nervous about ❓ sex: if ❓ is born a woman, she would want to be born in a "woman friendly" society.

Concerning sex, there is also the aspect of the lesbian, bi-sexual, trans-sexual, and gay (LBTG) population, who have been even more persecuted than women. For this reason (persecution), Wilder would much prefer being born heterosexual than LBGT. The world of LBGTs is a tough one.

Intelligence.

John Stewart Mill mused:

> *"It is better to be a human being dissatisfied than a pig satisfied; better to be Socrates dissatisfied than a fool satisfied."* (Crisp, 1998)

Superior intelligence, according to Mill, is what separates humans from animals, because of this he feels that persons would rather be intelligent human beings than satisfied animals. A person's intelligence might improve somewhat by hard work and study, but it is generally considered an inborn trait. Humans are born with varying degrees of intelligence and this does affect a person's life: superior intelligence makes it easier to get a desirable job, understand various subjects, solve problems, and assist with many other endeavors. ...but it doesn't necessarily make you a happier person.

Wilder would like to be born with at least a slightly above average intelligence, and would not want to be deficient in intelligence, even if it might mean a happier life.

Health. Overall good health, which includes mental health, the absence of birth deficiencies and diseases, a strong immune system, etc., is a trait all future humans desire; and is, of all the inborn attributes, the one that Wilder is the most nervous about. Without good health, life is a struggle. Personal health is both an inborn and acquired attribute: one may be born with certain handicaps or acquire them throughout a lifetime due to accident or disease. Wilder fervently hopes to be born healthy and without handicaps both because it portends an easier life, and if one is born healthy at least at the start of one's life, one need not worry as much about the drop-in society's policies concerning healthcare.

Other Attributes. Other attributes that will be given to Wilder by the creator include height, eye color, hair color, handedness, athleticism, rhythm, and artistic ability. As every human being is unique, the possibilities are limitless. Once a person has been dropped into a society and established his/her ambitions, these minor attributes can become major: as the example of a person currently living in the U.S. wanting to be a basketball player illustrates. Wilder is now only worried about the major attributes; race and skin color, intelligence, health, and sex.

What would matter to you as you await the first meeting with the creator? *Each one of us has been in Wilder's position, but we didn't know it, as we weren't conscious!*

The Drop-In Interview

From Wilder's experience in previous lifetimes, ❓ knows just how significant one's "drop-in" society is. People with very similar native traits generally lead entirely different lives, largely dependent on the characteristics of their drop-in society.

With some inborn traits, the consequences are inherently positive or negative (in any society to be born healthy is preferred to be born physically challenged); but with most traits the way a drop-in society reacts to your inborn traits is even more important. A neo-liberal capitalist society would be much less likely to aid the sick or handicapped than a welfare or socialist state. The consequences of other traits, such as race and sex, are determined to an even greater extent by one's drop-in society. A woman dropped into a Muslim state in the twenty-first century would have a much different outlook on life than a woman dropped into Sweden in the same period; being a black in the US before 1860 is a totally different situation than being a black dropped into Europe now.

There are five major factors that Wilder is worried about concerning the Creator's choice of ❓ next drop-in society: its communal values, the time-period of the drop-in, the economic situation of the society, its political situation, and the local (family, town, etc.) aspects.

Communal Values. The drop-in society conditions the way your life develops, it attempts (and in most cases, succeeds) to mold you into its preferred form: a communal society (Eskimo, American Indian, Communist) attempts to mold communal values; a warlike society (Greek Spartan, Germany of the 1930s and 40s) rewards traits such as courage, loyalty, and obedience. While capitalist societies encourage self-interest and individualism; welfare and socialist states foster a spirit of community, equality, and co-operation. The education systems of the various societies are the major players in the conditioning process by the way they teach history, ethical values, and vocational training; constantly molding the individual to fit society's values. They do not always succeed in the molding process, but they try and always have some effect. A person can make choices refuting society's wishes—but a society is usually able to mold most of its people into making most of the choices it, society, prefers.

Time-Period. Souls can be dropped into a body during any time-period: prehistoric, classical Greek or Roman, the Middle-Ages, ancient Chinese, twenty first century, or even the third millennium (we, in the 21st century are, hopefully, not the final civilizations). The drop-in time-period is significant, not necessarily meaning the later time periods are better (especially in our present age of nuclear weapons, climate change, and inequality), but some time periods are more preferred. Being dropped-in during a period in which the world is at peace is usually preferred to one in which the world is at war; a period of prosperity, preferred to one of depression; a period of freedom, preferred to one of oppression; a world free of epidemics, preferred to one of rampant disease. The historical period one is dropped into has important bearings on one's ease of life: indoor plumbing and showers were unheard of in the Dark Ages, while they are common in virtually all societies of the twentieth century; automobiles and airplanes were not even thought of in classical Greece: in current western societies, rightly or wrongly, they are considered necessities. These conveniences do not necessarily mean a better life, but most people who have enjoyed them would prefer not to give them up.

For the purposes of this experiment, the time periods of the drop-in societies will be from 1900 until 2020, as to make our thought experiment more relevant.

Local Society. As important to Wilder as the historical time of the "drop-in" is the actual local society, the one society out of the many that make up a being's world during any historical time-period. For example, during the time frame of the 19th century Wilder could be dropped into the English commercial society, the indigenous societies of the Native Americans, the Chinese society of that time, or any other society of that era. The possibilities are endless.

Aside from the historical period, and the society within that period, one's place within that society will also be determined. It is vastly different to be dropped into the pre-civil war south as a slave, then as part of a plantation owning family; or to be dropped into twentieth century Germany as an Arian, rather than a Jew; or in the 21st century United States as a poor black person in contrast to a wealthy white. Within this society is the specific family (or lack of family) situation a being is placed.

Economic Situation. There are two different elements to one's economic situation: the drop-in society's economic system, and one's personal economic position within that society.

A drop-in society could be capitalist, socialist, fascist, or welfare; as we will see, the placement of a being in one or another of these economic systems will have a profound influence on his/ her basic outlook on life. Does the economic system promote fairness (stressing economic equality), or freedom (stressing the freedom of individuals to do whatever they want with their money and/or power)? Is the society in general a wealthy or poor one?

One's specific situation within the economic system is also extremely significant; a being born into a homeless situation in a capitalist society will have a different outlook on life than a being born into a wealthy capitalist family; a being born on a communal Indian reservation will have different economic ambitions than a being born in an affluent suburb. In aristocratic societies the first-born male often has significant advantages over his siblings.

Political Situation. The political situation of the drop-in society has an immense effect on a being. What form of government will ❓'s drop in society have; monarchy, oligarchy, anarchy, democracy? Will this government allow free speech, free assembly, trial by law; will it promote equality; is there a "draft"—one can never feel "free" with a military draft hanging over their head; is there a constitution? How does the society make its choices; by the ballot, or by force? Those are some of the political possibilities of a drop-in society.

Social Commitments of the Drop-In Society. Different societies treat their sick and handicapped in different ways: some reject them altogether and let them fend for themselves, some even kill their handicapped to strengthen the "gene pool" (Germany in the 1930's and 1940's); other societies do everything within their power to ensure the handicapped lead a good life. Most societies lie somewhere between these extremes. Much of Wilder's nervousness revolves around ❓ personal individual health issues and the social health commitment of the "drop-in" society. Is there universal free healthcare, or does healthcare depend on one's job and/or financial status? Does one's drop-in society have up-to-date health care facilities; if so, are they available to all? Are there adequate medical personnel to treat the sick, injured, or handicapped? These are some of the healthcare concerns Wilder has.

At the second interview, the Creator determines a being's drop-in society. Wilder is more nervous about the second interview than the first, if that is possible.

There is nothing, nothing at all, that Wilder can do to influence the Creator, it is all up to chance… God… karma. This does not, however, take away Wilder's power to influence ❓ own existence. Even though Wilder is issued particular traits and born into a particular society, ❓ still has the freedom to choose how ❓ will react to the circumstances the creator bequeaths ❓ with.

CHAPTER **2**

Previous Lives

IN PREVIOUS LIVES Wilder has been in vastly different situations. A brief description of some of them will alert us to why this undefined soul called "Wilder" is so nervous prior to meeting with the Creator.

———∞———

Wilder the Slave

During this lifetime Wilder was endowed with exceptional intelligence and dropped-in a southern US state as a black female slave. The lifetime was a horrible one as she not only was exploited but realized that she was being exploited by beings less intelligent than she. Because of her dark-skin, her masters considered her part of an inferior species and treated her as an animal, not as a fellow sentient human being. While Wilder endured the worst of American colonial society because she was a slave, she realized that many "free" human beings of that era were not faring much better: since they were not dropped into landowning families of wealth and influence they suffered many of the same drawbacks as she did. As poor folk, the "free whites" also had little in the way of economic prospects—but at least they were treated as humans, although inferior ones.

The lucky beings of Southern society were dropped into prominent families that owned large plantations with numerous black slaves and poor whites (wage slaves) to work the land for them. Wilder did not see how the "free and equal" society of Thomas Jefferson (a slave owner) was at all fair: the slaves and the poor did all the work while the landowners derived all the benefits…it was "free and equal" only at the top!

Wilder especially resented being dropped-in with superior intelligence while having to be subservient to wealthier less-intelligent people. She would have preferred having inferior intelligence so as not to be as aware of the injustices she was suffering…but superior intelligence is what the creator endowed her with. Wilder resigned herself to her position in life, but was dedicated to the improvement of her lot and that of her fellow human beings—for this she was hanged during one of the slave uprisings of the 1840's.

Wilder could not understand why she… who, like us all, never asked to be born… was placed in a society that was as unfair as this one. Wilder once confronted the Creator with the question of "fairness in the process of creation," the Creator stated…" life is not created fair, but it could be made to be that way."

Wilder as a Gaucho

Another drop-in occurred in the pampas of Argentina where ❓ was created as a blind gaucho. During this lifetime Wilder learned the rigors of being self-sufficient. There were no other people within fifty miles and thus no help in case of sickness, accident, or any other misfortune. It was a hard, but rewarding life, Wilder—again having been endowed with above average intelligence—felt that he was living little more than the life of an animal, existing only to satisfy his appetites. Not interacting with humans outside of his immediate family, Wilder felt disadvantaged in his quest to develop his mental abilities because he lived in such an isolated area: he felt there must be more to life than just survival. He desired to be part of a larger society, one in which he could more fully develop as a human being. Wilder had a short life as a gaucho; the blindness he was given by the Creator contributed to his death when he was detached from a small group, became lost and eventually froze in the cold and snowy Argentine pampas.

Why was Wilder cursed by blindness and allowed to die a long painful death while other beings with all their senses intact could have saved themselves? Why was he "dropped-in" such a desolate area. Wilder felt that the manner that he was allocated native traits (especially his blindness) *was not fair,* and neither was his drop-in society since his blindness was correctable. In a wealthy, fair society he could have been treated by a government health care system, even though his family was poor. A fair society would have helped— after all it was not his fault that he was born blind— it was the creator's. Wilder wanted fairness, he got none; neither in his inborn traits or in the society in which he lived. Fairness would be a primary require-ment if Wilder were ever to design a society. Again, Wilder was not happy with the Creator.

Wilder on Wall Street

Another drop-in occurred in the US; this time Wilder was created as a male born into a wealthy, influential family, however, without the blessing (or curse) of superior intelligence. Wilder was a being of only average intelligence and did not question the morals of his society. Wilder was happy with this drop-in: He felt that with his "correct" up-bringing (following the manner of his social class by going to college, embracing the values of the US, being patriotic [but not so patriotic as to serve in the military… that was for others] and working hard at his chosen profession), he could fully develop himself and become "successful." After graduating from an "Ivy League" business school where he made many valuable "connections," he chose to pursue the career of a money manager, a profession that involved moving money in and out of third world countries as the financial markets dictated. Wilder was either not smart enough or didn't care enough to find out that the ramifications of his financial dealings created starving refugees out of third world populations.

What Wilder did know is that he was lucky to be dropped-in a country like the US; where everyone had fair opportunity, just as he had, and if they worked hard and followed the written and unwritten rules they could be "successful," that is, "make a lot of money." Wilder knew he could have become almost whatever he wanted; it never occurred to him that others were dropped-in without the favorable characteristics he enjoyed. He also never considered that making money might not be the best of all possible goals; Wilder was not a questioner, he thought his society's values were cast in stone for all to follow and making money was the only possible reason for living. Wilder died during the World Trade Center terrorist attack. He would never understand why he was the target of the terror attacks. He never realized that the people whose economies he had unknowingly destroyed did not condone either the system or the laws of western capitalism.

Cuba and Wilder

A much different drop-in occurred when Wilder was placed in Cuba as a female during the Castro regime. In Cuba race and gender make little difference in a being's life situation, since from the time of the Cuban Revolution (1959) almost all workers work for the state, and their wages are similar (none of the tremendous wage differences of the US economy are tolerated). In post revolutionary Cuba there is little private property...the state owns the means of production. One works (many times at a menial unfulfilling task) and by doing so fulfills his/her contribution to the economy: For this one receives a wage (or ration coupons) that entitles him or her to purchase the necessities of life that are not provided by the state. Since most necessities are produced and provided by the state (housing, food, clothing, health care, etc.), wages are correspondingly low and quite equal among all workers regardless of their profession. That is, all workers working at the same occupation (such as field workers like Wilder) are paid equally; workers with different types of jobs (even highly skilled workers such as doctors and engineers) are paid salaries quite similar to the field workers. Thus, doctors become doctors because they want to heal, not because they want to make inflated wages. *The Cuban system is based on economic equality, not individual freedom;* individual freedom in Cuba is subordinate to both economic equality and the needs of the state.

In Cuba the welfare of the state is deemed more important than that of the individuals in it. The state determines what is most needed by the public (whether it be sugar and soybeans, or electric garage door openers and cell phones. The state then produces it and prices the product at a level it deems fit; not necessarily to make a profit, but to assure that all are provided with the necessities of life. Cuba's economic system is not market-determined but planned for the best economic outcome for all…less economic freedom, more economic equality.

This system will not produce many of the marginally useful items (such as electronic games) but will produce necessities (such as food and housing). Rational production priorities are established by the state, not the market. A person in Cuba is responsible for his/her obligation to the state (work), he/she fulfills that obligation, and then is entitled to his/her basically equal share of the state's production.

There were, however, two problems Wilder was aware of. The first is that there is little incentive for working hard to improve one's situation, since everyone receives generally the same wage whether they work hard and put in extra time, effort, etc., …or goof off. This lack of incentive may be why the economic level of Cuba is so far below the economic level of its neighbor to the north. Second, if one wants to "get ahead" in Cuba the way is to join the "party" and control others, but that option wasn't open to all, nor was controlling other people an occupation that Wilder desired. For Wilder, there was some gratification working in the farm communes and making the "quota," but in the manufacturing sector where the jobs were repetitive and boring there was little enjoyment of, or incentive for hard work.

A third problem is that in Cuba there is little in the way of individual and political freedoms. People are afraid to speak out on controversial issues; in Cuba's one-party system, their vote is meaningless and Cubans have minimal legal rights against the government.

Wilder led an uneventful life in Cuba, but she was constantly aware of the lack of political and individual rights, and even though she had free health care, subsidized housing, and a guaranteed job as a sugar cane harvester; her life's situation was well below the *economic* standards of those living in the US, and the satisfaction of making the group quota did not seem to make up for the poor standard of living.

Wilder could not comprehend the morality of the US economy. She wanted to raise her economic position, but not at the expense of others, which seemed to be the norm in the competitive and greed infested US. How could the high economic standard of living that the US is said to have, be reconciled with the lack of medical care and homelessness that she heard is prevalent there, to say nothing of the economic inequalities—the US has some of the greatest economic inequalities in the world? In Cuba, as Che and Fidel said, "We are all in it together."

Wilder realized that the genuine difference in social structure between the US and Cuba is that in the US most people are concerned with their own well-being, while in Cuba the entire nation works together. Basic overall feelings are different in a capitalist than in socialist country: it is *we* in a socialist country while it is *me* in a capitalist one. Which system produces more…which leads to the greatest happiness… which is the fairest?

Wilder realized how dependent those to the North are as to what type of native traits they are endowed with and into what situation they are "dropped," since because of the capitalist economic system in the US, if you had more desirable native traits and were dropped into a promising economic and social situation, you would lead an economically fruitful life. But if you were born with less advantaged traits and into a poor family, you faced hardship and poverty. This is not so much the case in Cuba, where birth and drop-in characteristics are not as important because of the fairness of the socialist economic system. Although the sacrifices in human liberties and the difficulty of improving one's economic position in Cuba are great negatives, there is little inequality in income, and little severe poverty. Wilder still couldn't fathom that there were poor beings in the economically wealthy US, and that these poor, unlike Wilder, have minimal, if any, medical care and in some cases, are homeless. She was confused and needed to know which are more important, political freedom and personal economic advancement; or social cohesiveness and national economic welfare with restrictions on personal and political rights? Wilder felt the lack of political and individual freedoms and the low living standards found in Cuba were not good, but she also realized that the extreme competitiveness promoted by the basic structure of US society (inequality, feelings of alienation, loneliness, and despair, among the less fortunate) may be equally bad. Americans believe that all citizens should start out in life with an equal opportunity to "succeed," but the reality is that one's drop in situation is crucial to the determination of his/her economic level in that extremely unequal society.

Which system, Wilder wondered, was superior? *Might a reasonable economic situation, as in Cuba, be a basic human right as well as the personal and political rights so treasured in the US? Is capitalism a necessary step on the way to socialism, as Marx believed? Is a planned economy superior to a market economy, as the rulers of the former Soviet Union and many conservationists believe? Can we have both?*

Germany, 1933-1945

Wilder's most difficult and existential drop-in occurred as an intelligent, lower middle class, healthy, white German male, during the rise of Hitler. Throughout this era (the early to mid-1930's), the world was in a terrible state— after the conclusion of a devastating war, a worldwide depression was bringing economies to almost a complete halt. It was made even more severe in Germany because of the reparations the Treaty of Versailles forced upon the defeated WWI Axis powers. In Germany there was widespread unemployment, runaway inflation, and social unrest; creating conditions of anarchy. Into this void, as frequently happens, stepped a dictator, Adolf Hitler, and the fascist Nazi Party marching under the title of National Socialism. By creating scapegoats for Germany's dire state (saying that Jews and other inferiors brought the state down) and giving his nation a direction (the development of a master race and militarization of Germany), Hitler and the National Socialists (Nazis) gained control of the democracy then in place and turned it into a dictatorship.

Much of the philosophy of Fascism (National Socialism) comes from Frederic Nietzche; who believed not in fairness, but in the development of humanity to its utmost capacity by creating a master race (and/or civilization) of super-humans. In fascism and in Communism (as in Cuba) *the individual is subordinate to the state (in most western societies the state is supposed to be a servant of the individual)*, but in German Fascism the state's function is the creation of a master race, not creating economic equality as is the case in Communist countries. Nazis believe that some persons and races are superior and some inferior, and that the inferior should be used for the benefit of the superior. Among those inferiors were Jews, gypsies, gays, and others born with undesirable traits and/or deficiencies. They were blamed for the dilution of the genes required for the supremacy of the "master race;" they were the scapegoats for the deplorable conditions existing in Germany. Eventually the gypsies, Jews, and handicapped started disappearing.

Wilder did not believe in the concepts of fascism…that citizens are subservient to the state and the role of the state is bound to the welfare of the wealthy, the corporate… the master race. Wilder thought that the German people, if they bothered to discover the exterminations going on in their country, would agree with him: but most Germans never bothered, or were too scared to risk bothering, so the exterminations continued. Most Germans never even realized that the Jews and others were gone, *nor did they want to realize it . . . they blocked it from their minds.* Wilder, however, being intelligent, moral, and inquisitive, realized what was happening—these people were being exterminated!

Wilder, personally came to a crossroad when he was about to be drafted into the German army to fight for this reprehensible government; he was so against the Fascist state and its principles that he felt he could not report for duty. Wilder was in conflict with the basic structure of the society he lived in. Wilder felt that the correct thing to do was to speak out against the extermination camps and the theory of the master race, but the consequences were severe…death, not merely imprisonment as a conscientious objector to the war (as was the case in the US during its wars). Did he have the courage to die for his beliefs, would the sacrifice of his life be worth it, or would it be a meaningless gesture? That was for Wilder an existential, life-defining question.

In the end, Wilder decided that the risk of almost certain death was too great a risk to take for the unlikely possibility of influencing enough Germans that they were following an unjust, morally corrupt course. He decided to escape Germany through Switzerland, and eventually joined the French underground movement that was fighting against his former country, Germany. Wilder survived WWII and lived the rest of his life in his adopted country of France. After much sole searching, Wilder was satisfied with what he had done during that difficult time.

People do make choices that define their lives, but they can't make the choices the Creator makes for them; that is, their natural traits and drop-in society. Wilder certainly would have chosen a different drop-in society in this case.

Wilder as an American Indian

Wilder's favorite drop-in was as a male American Indian in the mid-1800's. This was a life of harmony, both with nature and with the other Indians comprising his surroundings. The Indians felt themselves part of nature, not dominating it or being dominated by it, but enmeshed in it. Nature was religion, religion was nature: nature and the Indians were one, a whole; the Indian tribes operated as a unit, rather than a composite of individual parts; they were societies of co-operation rather than individual competitions (Carter, 1976).

As a young Indian male Wilder was a hunter; his part of the whole was to provide meat for the tribe. Wilder knew and loved the animals he hunted: hunting to the Indians did not mean slaughtering for sport and trophy; it meant taking from nature only what was needed to provide for the tribe's needs while living in harmony with nature. Wilder loved being a hunter-provider and felt extremely lucky to be born healthy so as to be able to make his contribution to society. He felt sorry for those in his tribe that health-wise were not as fortunate as he, but the tribe provided for those less fortunate by caring for them plus giving them tribal positions in which they were useful, so they could lead meaningful lives. Wilder realized that everything possible was being done for those less fortunate than he, unlike his experience in the Argentine pampas.

Wilder felt lucky with this birth and drop-in. Why wasn't the Creator always so generous?

But Wilder's life as an Indian ended tragically. He and his family died during a forced relocation of his tribe from Tennessee to Oklahoma: forced by the white man who was intent on stealing the Indians' land. It was not fair that the white man, a recent imposer on the lands of the Indian, possessing a mindset of property ownership and domination, could take away lands that the Indians used communally, in harmony with themselves and nature. Not only did the white man take over these lands and "develop" them, he drove out Wilder's people, re-locating them thousands of miles from their homes and causing many to die in the process, including Wilder.

Does "might make, right?" Wilder didn't think so. Is life fair? Wilder also did not think so.

Wilder as a Russian Peasant

One of the most interesting but least enjoyable of Wilder's drop-ins occurred when ❓was dropped in as a male peasant near the Russian Empire city of St. Petersburg in 1905. During the next 20 years Wilder witnessed the destruction brought on by World War I, the Russian Revolution of 1917, and the Russian Civil War of 1917-1924. As a peasant, Wilder was drafted into the Russian Imperial Army and fought the German army until Russia's surrender to Germany in 1918. Wilder was a good soldier, but when the war was sure to be lost (at least for the Russians), and the Czar and his cronies were keeping Russia in the war solely to please their capitalist allies (Britain, France, and the US); Wilder, along with most of his fellow soldiers sided with the Revolutionary forces to over-throw the Czar and his Imperial government, end the war, and go home. Wilder then sided with the Bolsheviks (Red Army) who were advocating a socialist (Communist) government and economy. Communist socialism (Bolshevik socialism) was intended to mean a totally classless society governed by a strong one-party system, with the state totally controlling the economy. The Red Army fought the White Army which was composed of the Russian middle and upper classes that were opposed to socialism. When Wilder's army (the socialist Red army) won out, Wilder was ecstatic, for it seemed that the poverty-stricken peasants and industrial workers would get relief. Meanwhile, within the Bolshevik Party there developed a feud between the Bolsheviks, strict one-party advocates of immediate and total socialism, and the Mensheviks, who were more open to a gradual and democratic change-over. The Bolsheviks, under the sway of Lenin, won out, and the Communist party gained power. Wilder was for the Bolsheviks and was a supporter (although not a member of the Party). This was a mistake as the Bolshevik (Communist) Party turned into a dictatorship under Lenin, and later, Stalin. It was not a friendly dictatorship and was ruthless in its decimation of civil rights. Under the Bolsheviks it was the state that mattered (as in our Cuba example), not the people, and the state eventually became totally under control of the dictator, Joseph Stalin. Stalin ruled ruthlessly: he forcibly removed Wilder and his family from their home to a collective farm more than 200 miles away. During the forced march, many died: Wilder lost two of his children. But Wilder was fortunate: his brother, who was also a Bolshevik supporter, was executed along with his family, without a trial, when he was suspected of being disloyal. Millions died, or were executed under the "Stalinist purges," but somehow Wilder lived through them and fought again to save Stalingrad during World War II.

After WWII, in which the Union of Soviet Socialist Republics (formerly the Russian Empire) lost upwards of 8 million people, Stalin died, and the Communist Party became somewhat less of a dictatorship, but very much corrupt...still with little or no civil or political rights. There developed an "underground second economy," run as a capitalist economy in competition with the official socialist economy. Because it was "underground" (illegal), criminals were its main constituents. Wilder lived to see all of this. He was confused. Why did the Bolsheviks, who seemed to have good intentions, turn to a ruthless dictatorship condoning purges and forced relocations, with no protection of civil rights and no meaningful constitution? Why does this so frequently happen after popular uprisings (French and Spanish Revolutions)? Why after Stalin's death couldn't the Communist Party keep its good socialist economic policies and develop a Bill of Rights, instead of destroying its economic progress, eventually turning to a particularly corrupt form of capitalism? Why did Russia destroy the best of what it had, and incorporate the worst of the "western world?" It seemed to Wilder that Russia could just as easily have kept its own great social safety net, while incorporating the democratic human rights stances of the west.

Wilder died at the Berlin Wall trying to escape to the "free" west fearing the dictatorial government of the USSR...the utopian notions of Marx and Lenin's communism having fallen into the degenerate ruthlessness of the Communist Party.

CHAPTER 3

Thought Experiment (Part Two)

Waiting

WILDER IS WAITING in line for ❓ first session with the creator, ❓ surrounded by friends. As they pass the time chatting, the conversation turns to their approaching lives. The beings in line with Wilder are Pip, Vic, Beck, Lee, and Jan—each with their respective souls. The Creator doesn't have a direct influence on a person's soul, *a soul ultimately has control of* ❓ *thoughts and actions, and with it the responsibility for them;* but the Creator does have influence on the molding of souls by selection of the drop-in society.

The characteristics of the friends' souls are:

Wilder-inquisitive, always trying to find answers to the larger questions of life

Pip-socially oriented, concerned with the welfare of the less privileged

Vic – an individualist, self-reliant

Beck – oriented toward justice and/or the law

Jan – a family type, wanting things to "work out"

Lee – a pure "good" soul

Wilder poses a question: "In a situation such as we are in now—all of us being equal since we have yet to acquire our natural traits and do not know the advantages or drawbacks of our drop-in society; what values, customs, and laws would we enact if we could create our own society? What would most ease the terrible tension that we are experiencing? "

There was a silence, then Pip spoke up, "We are experiencing this tension because each of us is about to begin a whole new life, and none of us have any idea of what this life will be: we have no idea of our naturally endowed traits, or of the society we will be dropped into. How could we not be nervous?"

"But why aren't we all excited about the new lives we are about to enter? Why are we nervous instead of excited?" countered Wilder.

Lee answered," the reason is that for most of the earth's recent history the economic and social situation in general has been unfair. There are some exceptions to this trend, but in general, societies have been both unfair and unequal. The earth's natural resources have been plentiful enough and the capitalist system of production efficient enough to produce the basic needs for all beings, but this hasn't happened. The output of most of the prevailing systems of production and distribution has been under the control of the aristocracy, the extremely wealthy, and large corporations. Because of this, for us unborn beings too much depends on the creator's whim; that is, what natural traits God/chance bestows us with; and the drop-in society we are placed in. Characteristic of recent types of drop-in societies, a being's social position at birth determines the standard of living ❓ is attached to for life, and by means of social convention and inheritance laws, this status is usually passed on from generation to generation.

"The capitalist system has done a good job of producing enough goods for humanity to be provided with its basic needs, but this produce has not been distributed fairly; so much of the earth's resources are allocated to the top one-percent, or even the top one tenth of one percent, that the chances for the average person to live a fulfilling life are slim. The 'one per cent' enjoy privileges on both sides of the equation; on the production side by having better and more secure jobs, and on the consumer side by having the power to purchase more goods and services. In most of these societies the social safety net is slim, which puts the most vulnerable citizens at the highest risk. If the likely drop-in societies were fairer, and our chances of leading a fulfilling life were greater, we would be much less nervous."

"If the capitalist society is the most likely society to be dropped into, but the clear majority within that system are nonetheless impoverished, what is our likelihood of leading fulfilling lives," asked Vic.

"Not very good. There is little fairness or equality in this system, a system that has taken over the world's economy and threatens to take over its politics. In a capitalistic society, the majority are much more likely to end up poor and/or homeless than wealthy and powerful... our chances of even ending up in what is called the 'middle class" are receding. That is why we are worried," exclaimed Pip.

"I take it then, that in most situations you are more concerned about your drop-in society than your personal attributes," said Vic.

"That's right, since if you are dropped into a fair and just society (and there are some), there is less inequality and more social concern. If you are dropped into a fair and just society with unfavorable traits you can still lead a fulfilling life— and if you are handicapped, the effects of your handicap are minimalized by that society," replied Beck. "In an unfair society, even if you have favorable traits, unless you are dropped into the upper levels of this society you are likely to have a poor life experience. Unfortunately, the likelihood of being dropped into the upper realm of this type of society is at best 100 to 1 against you."

"That's correct," said Pip, "and since our likelihood is to be dropped into the unfair and unequal capitalist societies of 1900-2020, I am extremely nervous. I am nervous because of the healthcare, economic, racial, and sexual issues in these unfair societies; and unhappy that the traits needed to succeed in these type societies (greed, self-interest, lack of empathy, etc.) are not the kind of traits I value."

They were silent for a while until Pip spoke, "Since the chances of being dropped into the top strata of a wealthy society are slim in comparison to the chance of being dropped-into a poor society in a lower social-strata; I would give up my ambitions of wealth and power for the assurance that my drop-in society would be a fair, just, and caring one that provides conditions that enable me to meet my basic needs. If after the interviews I knew that I would be endowed with favorable traits along with a favorable drop-in, I might think differently; but not now, when I don't know my innate make-up or drop-in society, where the chances of a favorable outlook are slim. I can't bear the thought of living as a French peasant again before the revolution; with no individual rights or freedoms and no hope of improving my lot in life (the French feudal society being a wealthy, but unjust society).

"I agree," replied Beck, "I too would not want to risk being impoverished and repressed in an unfair society for the slim chance of leading an ideal life in its upper strata. I would rather take my chances with a more equal welfare or socialist society— where the lower echelons of society fare reasonably well —since the chances of being in the upper echelons of a capitatist society are remote. I want to be certain that my basic needs are met and that I can look forward to a fulfilling life in whatever path I choose." They all agreed that *while in the original position where we are all equal,* fairness and some security are what we desire, rather than the slim chance of being born into wealth and power.

"Thinking that we will be dropped into a fair and just society is what would ease our tensions prior to the drop-in interview, but now we are not experiencing that feeling because our probable drop-in societies are in the 1900-2020-time period," commented Pip, "a time period in which there are a preponderance of unfair societies...and few with adequate social safety nets."

Wilder continued, "Now that we realize what the main cause of our anxiety is, what could be done to change our expectations to relieve the anxiety?"

"Obviously we need to better our chances of being dropped into a fair and just society that has the ability to fulfill our basic needs," replied Pip.

"It follows then, that for us to create, or even imagine, the society we want when we are in *the original position,* we need to determine two things related to drop-in societies: what are our basic needs that must be fulfilled, and what type of society would fulfill them," added Vic.

Basic Needs

"Obviously, the most basic needs are food, shelter, and health care," offered Vic, "you can't live without these needs being fulfilled."

"I agree that food, shelter, and health care are basic needs; but we are all involved in society whether we like to admit it or not. Most beings in this era (1900-2020) do not make their own clothes or grow their own food; basic needs are met by specialization in production and utilizing society's free market system for both production decisions and distribution of goods and services. How could a being be certain that the basic needs you mentioned would be provided if there weren't a governmental system responsive enough to its citizens to enable this to happen? You're putting the cart in front of the horse, one can't just say I want this or I want that; there needs to be a just and fair *system* in place that will provide these necessities—free market or otherwise. Even more important is the question as to whether you feel that the economic needs you mentioned take precedence over individual rights and freedoms such as free speech and association, religious freedom, the right to fair and equal treatment before the law, the right to freely pursue your chosen work and way of life, not be unjustly imprisoned or searched, and the right to have some influence over your government either by the ballot or by other methods?

People have fought and died rather than give up these rights! Would a life even be worth living if these individual rights, freedoms, and privileges aren't protected? Political and individual rights should have priority over the economic and survival needs you suggested, since if you don't have the political rights, you won't have a fair system to produce and distribute the economic ones, and without at least the most basic personal rights and freedoms, life might not be worth living," replied Beck.

"That's not true!" answered Vic, "If I were starving would I care about personal or political rights? No, I would want food and shelter to survive, the rest would be superfluous."

"But is it? I don't think so, on two accounts," countered Beck, "In the first place, would you feel that your life is worth living if you're constantly worried about being carted off to prison, having your home searched, being conscripted into a war you don't believe in, or worried about being forcibly sent off to work in a place such as Siberia? That happens if you don't have political and individual rights," Beck continued, "that's the prime reason for my belief in the over-riding importance of a just and fair government. The second reason is economic.

"We live on a planet with enough resources to adequately house, feed, and clothe its entire population; people do not have to be starving in this world, but they are. We shouldn't have to worry about simple survival, but because of the systems (both political and economic) established in most of the present world ...we do worry. Our problem does not presently concern survival in a world of drastically limited resources, but survival in a world of only moderate scarcity. What is needed are correct political and economic systems to ensure that necessities are provided now, *and that the environment is protected for our future lives.*"

"Some of what you say, Beck, may be true, but I certainly would give up a few of my political rights, such as the right to vote, which is almost meaningless in a large manipulative society, to fulfill more essential survival needs," replied Vic.

"Vic, I agree with you to a degree, but you're looking at the question from a narrow point of view. What if everyone who was down and out gave up their right to vote, then *a responsive* government would not hear their point of view and their interests eventually would be suppressed?"

"But what if the political process is arranged so you only *think* your vote means something, such as when in a two-party system both parties represent basically the same thing and the people want something different; or there are irregularities in the voting process; or wealth and power control the election's results? In cases like this, does your right to vote matter?" countered Vic.

"On this point, Vic, I will have to agree with you. If a democracy is not real, then your vote doesn't matter. We are concerned with *real democracy and real individual rights*...when elections are rigged, bought, or the parties represent the same thing, your vote is meaningless."

"I am still not convinced of the precedence of political over economic rights in a society," stated Vic, "if I don't have enough food to eat, clothes to wear, or a place to live, what does that leave me with?"

Beck countered, "Let me give you a few examples of what can happen when economic policies usurp political and individual rights as they did during the reign of terror in the wake of the French Revolution, the Five-Year Plans of Russia's Stalin, and the Communist dictatorship of Cuba. In each of these instances increased economic equality was a main goal, but both economic and political disaster followed.

In the case of the French Revolution anarchy reigned and there were wholesale convictions and executions for treason without proper trials, culminating with the eventual takeover of French government by Emperor Napoleon. After the Russian revolution, there was also chaos. Eventually Lenin and later Stalin ruled, not democratically, but as dictators; there were mass slaughters and millions of deaths caused by the forced relocation of peasants in the attempt to rearrange the Russian economic system. Those in power were reluctant to give up their power, and although the government apparatus according to Communist doctrine was supposed to "wither away," it didn't, and the Russian people suffered through dictatorship for over fifty years resulting in millions of unjustified deaths. In Cuba after its revolution although the effects were milder, there were the same displacements of populations, lack of justice, and failure to relinquish power as there were in Russia...all in the name of economic equality."

"But didn't the benefits of a more economically equal society make up for this?" asked Pip.

"Because of the faulty political system, the economic systems of these countries failed to produce, and their economies faltered; so even though people were more equal, almost all had less. But even if that were not the result, even if the economic systems of these countries produced enough to reasonably feed, clothe, and house their populations, would you want to be ruled in this manner? Think about it, could you live where there was either no justice, or a very arbitrary judicial system... systems in which you never had any personal security, could be displaced or conscripted at any time, and had no say whatsoever in how your government was run?" replied Beck.

Wilder again assuming the role of moderator, replied, "I agree with you, individual and political rights are more important than economic ones. For a just society to work, political and individual rights must trump economic ones."

> "Basic individual or political rights cannot be compromised by economic ones; they can only be compromised if they are in conflict with more important individual or political rights."
>
> (Rawls, 2001).

As the discussion progressed they realized that for them to feel comfortable in their present pre-birth situation (the original position), they all wanted their future society to be just and fair, and the differences in traits they were endowed with by the creator be minimized by the constructs of society. Their reasons for feeling this way were selfish reasons rather than benevolent ones, as they all realized that their chances of a decent drop-in society are minimal and they wanted to ensure a decent life for themselves.

Wilder, again the moderator, reminded them that "even though economic rights and privileges are relegated to a position secondary to individual and political rights, they are nonetheless a major concern. One can't be content if ❓ is not financially secure. How should economic rights be handled?"

Pip, the friend with the social conscience, replied, "I know that many of us would want to be in the higher social strata of an advanced society, but the odds are heavily against this…would you like to gamble on your chances in an unfair, unequal society; or be dropped into a more equal and fairer society, one in which the odds of having the necessities of life are much greater, but the chances of being extremely well off are much less?"

"To be comfortable in our present condition (the original position) I would need to know if there are enough natural resources available for everyone to have the necessities; if there are not enough resources, everyone should be provided for equally. After we are all ensured of the necessities, we should be able to pursue whatever we feel is a good life," replied Wilder.

In a previous life Pip had lived through the great depression of the 1930's and experienced the hunger and grief of the world during it. Witnessing the depression greatly affected Pip—who could only feel good in a society in which there was at least the hope of freedom from hunger, homelessness, extreme medical expenses, and poverty for everyone. Pip believed that in a fair and just society economic rights are required, as well as individual and political rights. Economic necessities should either be provided for or be within the means of all citizens. Each citizen should be entitled to a fulfilling job, and no one should be allowed to amass a great amount of wealth *until all* are provided with at least the basic economic necessities: *the*

basic welfare of all should come before extravagant pursuits of a few.
Pip remembered that after the depression of the 1930's, the US president, Franklin Roosevelt, was in the process of proposing a "Second
Bill of Rights" (Sunstein, 2004) which included *economic* rights, such
as the right to a productive job, food to eat, adequate health care,
education, and reasonable housing. Pip thought this was a good start
to a fair and just society. The friends agreed with Pip.

The group's preference for a society concerned with fairness
seemed clear: *they all preferred the security of being inserted into
a fair and just society rather than taking their chances on what their
social position and natural attributes would obtain for them in an
unfair one.*

What constitutes a fair and just society?

Vic felt that social programs should not be free, because without
the prospect of benefiting from one's own hard work little would be
accomplished. ❓ felt that if there were extensive social safety nets
there would be little incentive to work, since almost all a person's
needs would be provided. Inequalities arising from the development
of one's native traits through hard work and dedication result in im-
provements for the whole of society; incentives for hard work and
creativity are beneficial to all society. Vic was opposed to welfare.

"There need to be incentives to better ones-self; rewards for hard
work, inventiveness, and all other actions that help both the individual and the community. All should have an equal opportunity to obtain
these rewards, that is, everyone should start off with equal economic
opportunities and by one's own energies be able to improve their lot
in life." *Equality for Vic meant equality of opportunity.* Vic didn't want
to be dropped in with less than equal economic opportunity (such
as having no inheritance, while others had millions, or having little
opportunity for a good education while others are assured of one),
but Vic didn't want government giveaways either. ❓ thought that by

expending extra effort and/or possessing superior natural traits, it is fine for individuals to live above the norm. Everyone, Vic felt, should start with an equal chance of economic success, then it is up to each being to fend for itself and produce. Vic didn't have much use for the pleasures and rewards of communal and/or cooperative ventures that brought benefits to all without much regard for who worked hard, and who didn't. Vic was an individualist.

Beck raised questions; one of them being that *since all beings' innate traits are not equal (we all can't be a seven-foot-tall basketball star, or have Einstein's brain), even in a society that grants equal opportunity we would never have an equal chance for success: those lucky enough to have been born with desirable traits would likely, with no more (or even less) effort than the rest of us, succeed in cases where the less endowed would fail. Is that fair...just?* If a being with lesser natural traits was dropped-into a society advocating only equal opportunity; could he or she succeed, even with hard work? Maybe...but probably not. To feel comfortable with your drop-in society, something more than equal opportunity is needed.

Could "affirmative action," a term Pip had come across in a previous life as a 1970's black woman in New York, be the answer?

During that drop-in Pip was an underprivileged black woman, who, because of affirmative action, was granted benefits that enabled her to attend a university and succeed in providing for the economic needs of her family. The extra support given to some blacks applying for college was said to be justified because of their previous persecutions, lack of wealth, and unequal prior education. During that life, affirmative action greatly improved Pip's chances for a decent life...she appreciated affirmative action.

Beck informed them that this may have been at the expense of a more qualified, intelligent, white person— *affirmative action conflicts with equality before the law!* Which of these rights should prevail— fairness or equality, or could they both be provided in a fair and just society?

Vic persisted; ❓ felt that it is only right that if one person worked harder than another, that person should be allowed to reap the benefits of their hard work and economic benefits that resulted; but also realized that this would only be fair if both were created with equal native traits and inserted into a society that enforced equality of opportunity.

Pip also persisted; Pip felt that, hard work or not, individuals were dropped-in with different traits and different social rankings, thus a poor person with low intelligence would have to work much harder than an intelligent, wealthy, white, to get ahead; and this was not fair. Beck did not give in either; ❓ felt that treating the poor or handicapped differently than the healthy and wealthy flew in the face of equality provisions previously discussed, plus it would cast a negative light on those taking advantage of affirmative action programs.

A three-way conflict developed between equality of opportunity (Vic), affirmative action (Pip), and equality before the law (Beck). How was this to be resolved?

---∞---

Conflict

Pip suggested, "For us all to be treated fairly, those disadvantaged by the creator should be given a little extra, a head start, so that they could compete with the advantaged on a more even plane. Think about it again, what would we desire at this point as creatures about to be dropped-in? (*If the Creator were to give us all the exact same traits, this problem wouldn't arise, but that is not the case, we are all created as unique human beings with our very own set of native qualities*. This presents us with the problems we are now considering: some having traits more beneficial than others."

"I would like not to have to worry so much as to what traits and drop-in society the Creator provides me with; if a drop-in society had a process like affirmative action, these worries would be moderated," said Pip.

"Yes, they would," replied Beck, "but is it fair not treating everyone equally? In addition to the charge that affirmative action may be unfair because everyone is not treated in the same manner (some getting the "head starts" that others don't), wouldn't this type of policy lead to the social stigmatization and resentment of those receiving the benefits from those who don't?"

"Maybe," replied Pip, "maybe not."

"Let me clarify this quandary. We have to choose between equality of opportunity, affirmative action, and equality before the law," declared Beck.

"That's correct, unless we can find another way," replied Wilder.

Solution

It was then that Jan who had been silent till now, expressed ❓ idea. "Instead of affirmative action, what if those that worked harder could reap the benefits of their hard work and economically advance *as long as the economic benefits that accrued to them were distributed throughout society?* This would eliminate the 'equality' problems concerned with affirmative action. The person who worked hard to obtain economic advantages above the minimum would be entitled to live above the norm, but those below the norm would benefit also, although not from the direct handouts and privileges associated with affirmative action, but by taxes which would spread the wealth throughout the society."

"You mean to use taxation to rectify social problems in addition to its function of funding of the government?" asked Pip.

"That's exactly what I mean," said Jan, "using taxes to level the playing field will go a long way to reducing inequality. *Raising money to fund governments doesn't have to be the only function of taxation… redistribution of wealth and income should also be a function.*"

"That does seem a fair and just method," admitted Vic, "and it will encourage the less economically advantaged to hope for the success of the more financially gifted; with the added social value of every-one wanting everyone else to succeed, as the benefits are shared?"

"That is true," cited the socially conscious Pip, "it could make for a society of teammates, but how could a tax system accomplish this?"

"That is what we need to work out," cried Jan.

They all liked this approach; it seemed a workable one. The group now felt that they could welcome being dropped-into this type of society *even if they did not know what their inherited traits or social position would be*—a just and fair theory, at last!

CHAPTER 4

Taxation

The Difference Principle

> *Social and economic inequalities should be arranged so that inequalities are expected to be to everyone's advantage, with the least advantaged benefiting the most. The distribution of wealth and income, and positions of authority are to be consistent with the basic liberties and equality of opportunity.*
>
> (John Rawls 2001)

Income Tax Basics

Jan went on to explain that taxing everyone at the same fixed rate would not work, "Equal percentages would accrue more to the wealthy since the absolute value of their after-tax income would increase exponentially as they became wealthier and wealthier, while what they gave up to taxes would be so split among the poor that it would dissipate into a negligible sum."

Income	Tax (flat rate of 20%)	After tax income
30,000	6,000	24,000
100,000	20,000	80,000
1,000,000	200,000	800,000

As can easily be seen from this chart, the after-tax income of the million-dollar earners provides them with an enormous amount of money to become even wealthier, and the tax money provided to the populace is meager in comparison. A "flat-tax" will not work.

It was Beck who came up with what was the final saving argument. Beck felt that, "the entrepreneur or hard worker who managed to obtain economic gains should be allowed to keep them—as long as the poor obtained a *greater* gain than ❓ did. This could be accomplished by *a progressive tax.*"

"Are you serious," exclaimed Vic, remembering that there was a progressive tax on income of 91% after WW II in the US, "who would want to work harder or invest money if most of it were given up to taxes, certainly not me!"

"You're absolutely right, Vic, there would not be much incentive to work if that was the case, but you may have a misconception of progressive taxing, people can still become wealthy, but not extremely wealthy.

"This is the way it works:"

"First let's assume a poverty level of $40,000, and that anyone earning below that level would pay no tax at all, there would definitely be an incentive to work at this level since you could keep all you earn."

"Next, say that the tax rate is 20% on income between $40,000 and $100,000; then every person earning up to $100,000 would be liable for $12,000 in taxes (no tax required on the first $40,000 of income, but $12,000 on the $60,000 of income between $40,000 and $100,000). That would leave a person in this situation with $88,000 after tax income. This person would also have a reasonable incentive to work.

"Then say that if a person earns between $100,000 and $1,000,000; that person would be charged 60% on their earnings *between* $100,000 and $1,000,000. That person would pay $12,000 + $540,000 (60% of 900,000), for a total of $552,000 in taxes, and an after-tax income of $448,000. At this tax-rate some people would be inclined to work for the monetary reward involved, and others may not.

"Above this point (or at some other arbitrary point) the government might say enough income is enough, and tax the amount earned over $1,000,000 at 90%, so that a person earning $21,000,000 will pay $18,552,000 in taxes and have an after-tax income of $2,448,000, significantly more than $448,000, but is it worth the extra effort? In my opinion, no, but people in this high-income group are probably working for reasons other than financial benefits; such as power and prestige. Whatever the reason for these high incomes, taxing this 'excess income' benefits society, and hopefully through social programs the least well off benefit the most. At the very least, a progressive tax system levels the financial playing field.

Tax Table

Reflecting the above figures

tax rate	<40,000 no tax	40,000-100,000 20% tax rate	100,000-1,000,000 60% tax rate	over 1,000,000 90% tax rate
income equals	40,000	100,000	1,000,000	21,000,000
Less	0	0	0	0
a person with a 40,000 income takes home...	40,000	-12,000	-12,000	-12,000
a person with a 100,000 income takes home		88,000	-540,000	-540,000
a person with a 1,000,000 income takes home			448,000	-18,000,000
a person with a 21,000,000 income takes home				2,448,000

"Would this still give you the incentive to work hard and/or invest in risky undertakings?" asked Vic.

"It did in the 1950's. In the US there were no shortage of applicants for CEO's of our major companies back then, or for entrepreneurs," replied Beck,"there are other benefits accorded to executives beside pay: status, prestige, and power also factor in."

Beck continued, "There are various aspects of taxation; progressive income tax is not the only focus, there also needs be a progressive tax on <u>wealth</u>, as accumulation of excessive wealth (which is still possible, but much more difficult) can occur even with a progressive income tax). Excessive wealth needs to be curbed and shared in the same manner as excessive income, by taxing it directly, or by an inheritance tax. In our following conversation, we should assume that wealth taxes and property taxes are treated in similar manners.

Regressive Taxes

A regressive tax is one that benefits the rich rather than the poor. Examples of this type tax are:

Sales taxes on necessities such as food (since these necessities take up a greater proportion of a poor person's budget than a wealthy person's budget).

Taxes with a "cap" (an upper limit). An example of this is the notoriously unfair US Social Security tax. The current SS tax on an employee's income is 4.2% of income up to $120,000. There is no tax on an employee's income over $120,000. This means that an employee earning $120,000 pays $5,040 in SS taxes, while a manager earning $1,000,000 pays the same $5,040 in taxes. Regressive taxes have no place in a just and fair society.

CHAPTER 5

Basic Structure of a Society

BUT JAN STILL had some doubts stemming from this passage in John Steinbeck's novel, *Cannery Row:*

> *"It's always seemed strange to me," said Doc, "the traits that we admire in men; kindness and generosity, openness, honesty, understanding and feeling are the concomitants of failure in our system. And those we detest; sharpness, greed, acquisitiveness, meanness, egotism, and self-interest are the traits of success. And while men admire the quality of the first they love the produce of the second."*
>
> —John Steinbeck (1945)

Jan thought that it was true that the laws and direction of this society "seemed" correct, but ❓ realized that much of the society (the economic sector) would still be motivated by the greed of those that wanted to "get ahead." Jan felt that although the laws of society might be correct ones, *the structure of that society would still be based on the selfish economic traits.* ❓ did not feel greed was what was wanted as a motivator.

At that point, Lee spoke. "Beings are born with souls whose tendencies can be good, bad, or somewhere between: these tendencies can be affected by the society and/or logic. If a being with a good soul is dropped-in a greed-infested environment, such as that of Wall Street, then he or she in trying to conform to what is considered 'good' in that environment may come to view greed as a 'good.' In the opposite instance, when a being born with a tendency toward greed is dropped into an economic society such as the one we are proposing, that being might develop compassion and fairness in conformance to the general attitude.

"The laws promoted by basic individual and political rights, along with progressive income and wealth taxes, should distribute society's wealth and mold the *society's basic structure* to promote the values of human rights, equality, fairness, dignity, and teamwork; while the basic structure of the society in turn should mold future laws to conform to the concept of fairness.

"The basic social structure of a society determines, reflects, and builds the overall temperament of its people: selfishness, greed, love, anxiety, compassion, empathy, etc. Rights and laws are part of this structure as are religions, educational institutions, economic and political systems, and social mores—all societies do not have to conform to the greed and consumerism of laissez-faire capitalism. If we aspire to a more compassionate, just, and fair society, we must mold our social institutions, as well as our laws, to this end.

When the structure of the society reinforces its laws and its laws reinforce its basic structure, then a stable, long lasting society evolves: if this is a fair, just, and compassionate society, then we will have a stable, ideal, drop-in society. Deviations from our new society's morals are not forbidden, but the general tendency is towards justice and fairness, not greed and wealth. I believe that a constitutional democracy with a progressive tax system is the answer."

BOOK II

CHAPTER **6**

The Two Principles of Justice

AS THE TIME for their meetings with the creator grew closer, the group's thinking became more hands-on. Because of their emphasis on social justice they preferred to be dropped into a constitutional and democratic political society, with an economic system that prevents the accidents of dispersal (natural traits and advantages of social position) from determining the outcome of one's life. They wanted civil and political liberties and a society with less chance of becoming wealthy, but a greater chance of having one's basic needs satisfied; rather than one in which you could become extremely wealthy, but with a high chance of living in poverty.

They hoped to be dropped-into societies based on the following Rawlsian axioms:

- *Each person is to have an equal right to the most extensive system of basic liberties compatible with a similar system for all; and the loss of freedom for some cannot be justified by benefits to others.*
- *"Social and economic inequalities should be arranged so that inequalities are expected to be to everyone's advantage, with the least advantaged benefiting the most."*

- *They realized that since they are souls capable of being dropped into any society at any time, the societies they are dropped into must be environmentally sustainable; that is, the society must not waste the earth's resources, or pollute the environment...possibly making their future lives untenable.*

(Rawls, 2001)

The friends discovered from beings who had finished their second interviews that they were in a group destined for the time-period of 1900-2020. What types of societies were existing at that time, what types would they want to be dropped-into... what will their natural traits be, what will be left of the earth's resources; (remember always that they are viewing the systems and societies from the original position)? They were thankful that they still had some time together to discuss their hopes and fears concerning the lives they were about to begin. From their first interviews, they knew that they all were created as average human beings with no exceptional abilities and no outstanding disabilities.

In the time between their interviews and drop-ins they are allowed two days to "mentally adjust." Usually this time was absorbed by self-examination and meditation, but this time they decided to research possible drop-in societies and discuss their feelings about them. The way they decided to go about their research was: first, find countries that they would be *most likely* to be dropped into and research them; next, if time allowed, research some other societies they thought interesting.

When they researched world population statistics they discovered the following graph:

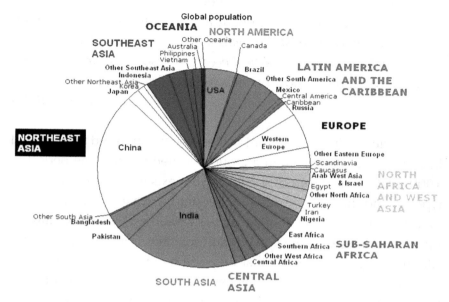

Source: Global Issues, Poverty Facts and Stats

From this graph, the group surmised that there is about a 70% chance of being dropped into China, India, Europe, or the United States; and a 30% chance of being dropped into the remainder of the world. They decided to research these most likely drop-in societies and a few others that interest them to see how each stood up to their principles.

They also wanted to have some idea of the overall poverty in the world to get an idea of their chances of living a decent economic life. They discovered that almost half of the world is living on less than $2.50 per day...*extreme* poverty!

From the following graph they determined that only 300 million persons out of the world's approximately 6 billion inhabitants earn over $20,000 per year (½ of 1 per cent). That makes a being's chances 1 in 200 to make more than $20,000 per year; and in the US and Britain that is considered below the poverty level.

World Income Distribution

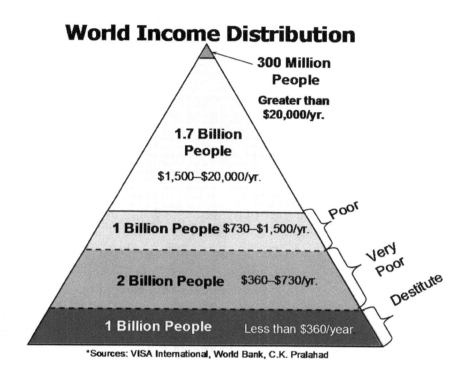

300 Million People

Greater than $20,000/yr.

1.7 Billion People

$1,500–$20,000/yr.

Poor

1 Billion People $730–$1,500/yr.

Very Poor

2 Billion People $360–$730/yr.

Destitute

1 Billion People   Less than $360/year

*Sources: VISA International, World Bank, C.K. Pralahad

"That seems impossible," voiced Pip.

"It sure does!" exclaimed Beck.

"The odds against being in the privileged class of the world's income level are astronomical, and this doesn't even put one out of the 'poverty' category in the US and western Europe. It is even more shocking when we know that there are enough resources in the world for us all to be provided with the essentials of life. *What is wrong?*" exclaimed Jan!

"I'm not so sure that I want to be dropped in at all," exclaimed Pip.

"Neither do we," voiced Scottie and Orion, newcomers to the group. "We just finished lives in Scandinavia, where all was plentiful and fairly divided. There are other places on earth during the time-period allotted to us that are like Scandinavia, but you need to be very lucky to be dropped into any of them...extremely lucky. With all the resources at the disposal of human beings, why is it so unlikely to be dropped into a decent lifestyle?"

"Beats me!" exclaimed Pip." Maybe most humans are programmed to be greedy, or simply to not care enough to be fair, conserve the environment, and work toward correcting unjust situations?"

"I've never heard of any souls being dropped into Scandinavia," said Pip, "even though our chances of being dropped in there are almost nil, I would like to investigate Scandinavia to find out why you had such a favorable life there."

The group decided to research Sweden, a Scandinavian country.

After much debate, these are the countries they decided to research, and why:

- India-because its population makes it a likely drop-in society
- China-because its population makes it a likely drop-in
- Saudi Arabia-because of its abundance of oil and its dictatorial government
- Sweden-because of the good report of the Scandinavian countries by Orion and Scottie
- Cuba-because it is neither democratic, nor capitalist, and has a planned economy
- Russia-because of its exceedingly interesting 20th and 21st century history
- France-because it is an influential European nation
- USA-because during this time frame the US was the most powerful country on earth

Because of their previous discussion concerning the superiority of individual and political rights, they decided to compose a list of those rights and freedoms that would be prerequisites if a society were to be considered "just and fair." They agreed that if a society they review comes up short on these rights, it does not conform to their theory of justice no matter what its economic system is.

Individual and Political Rights and Freedoms

To understand what individual and political rights and freedoms are required for a country to be considered, the souls had to make themselves familiar with the following political terms:

Bill of Rights. The fundamental rights and privileges guaranteed to the people against infringement by the state.

Constitution. The basic principles and laws of a nation detailing how it is governed; a constitution is almost always in written form (in some cases [England] it is a combination of documents). Although a constitution is necessary for determining an individual's rights and freedoms, having a constitution does not in itself guarantee these rights and freedoms. A constitution (as with Bills of Rights) must be enforced... not ignored.

Anarchy. A type of society which does not recognize authority.

Monarchy. A form of government in which the head of government is embodied in one individual who reigns until death; power is then passed on in a pre-determined manner to his or her descendants.

Constitutional Monarchy. Usually a monarchy in name only, with the monarch performing only ceremonial functions while the state is run by a democratic government (England).

Autocracy. A society in which an individual rules without any limits to his/ her authority: an absolute monarchy, a dictatorship... Hitler during WWII.

Totalitarianism. A political system in which the state holds total control over society and seeks to control all aspects of public and private life: Examples are Fascist Italy and Germany during World War II, and the Soviet Union under Stalin.

Oligarchy. A political system in which all power is held by a few persons or a dominant class; government by the few.

Plutocracy. A form of oligarchy in which power is held by a small group of wealthy people.

Liberalism. (very misunderstood and misused term emphasizing freedom): Aside from "neo-liberalism," liberalism is generally associated with the "left."

Classical liberalism. A political system that advocates civil liberties, along with economic and political freedom.

Neo-liberalism. A form of liberalism that desires to keep government as small as possible and allows corporations the "freedom" to do whatever they want with their money and power, but takes away the "freedom" of workers to move across borders, form unions, become educated, etc.

Social liberalism. A political system that seeks to balance individual liberty and social justice. It, along with classical liberalism and neo-liberalism, endorses a market economy with individual and political rights; but social liberalists believe that part of a government's function is the economic welfare of its citizens. Social liberalism is personified by President Franklin Roosevelt's "Four Freedoms" and "Second Bill of Rights." (Sustein, 2004)

Be careful that you know what people mean when they call themselves "liberal," as they may be any of the above.

Conservatism. A political and economic system that favors freemarkets, free trade, deregulation of business and environmental restrictions, inequality, law and order, immigration restrictions, less government, and state's rights. Conservative values are considered as being from the "right."

The Left and the Right. In politics and economics there is constant talk of "the left," and "the right." According to popular history the terms left and right derived from the seating arrangements of the legislature during the early phase of the French Revolution, taken from the point of view of the speaker. Over the years specifics have changed slightly, but the individuals on the speaker's left generally desire equality, large government, and extensive democracy; while those on the right are tolerant of greater inequality, want limited government, and restrictive democracy, plutocracy, or authoritarianism.

The "right." Holds the values of conservatism (see page 98)

The "left." Holds the values of socialism and the welfare state (see page 98)

Democracy. There are different types of democracy; all types proclaim government by the people and are associated with rule of the majority. Democracy types are:

Direct Democracy. A democratic system in which all laws are decided by a general vote of the citizens (the New England "town meeting"): one citizen, one vote.

Representative Democracy. A form of democracy in which citizens vote to elect representatives who wield power in their name. A republic is a form of representative democracy (most current nationwide democracies are of this form as national populations are too large to have direct democracy in their everyday workings).

Two Party Democratic System. A democracy where two major political parties dominate the politics of a country (contemporary USA is closest to this form, although the US is considered by some to be a plutocracy).

Multiparty Democracy. A form of democracy in which multiple political parties enter elections with legitimate chances of winning delegates (a multi-party democracy is almost always considered in conjunction with proportional representation-see below pg 54): all parties have a similar chance of gaining control either alone or in coalition with other parties (France).

Branches of democratic governments. (in some countries the legislative and executive branches are combined to form a parlimentary system).

> Legislative — branch that makes the laws
> Executive — branch that enforces the laws
> Judicial — branch that interprets the laws

Presidential system. A form of democratic government in which each of the branches is separate; where the people, or their representatives vote for both the President and congressional representatives. In some cases, judges are appointed; in others, elected.

A semi-presidential system. A system in which a president exists alongside a prime minister and cabinet, with the prime minister and cabinet responsible to the legislature. This differs from a parliamentary

system in that it has a popularly elected head of state (the president)...
and from a presidential system in that the cabinet and prime minister
are responsible to the legislature.

Parliamentary system. A form of democratic government in which
the legislative branch is voted for by the people and then that legislature elects a leader (usually the head of the dominant party) who be-
comes the country's executive (prime minister). He/she is not directly
elected by the citizens but by the parliment.

Majority Winner election. A person needs over 50% of the vote to
win an election.

First Past-the-Post/Plurality Winner election. A person needs to
have only the highest total of votes to win an election, not nesessarily
over 50%.

Winner take all elections. Election systems that award seats (or
votes) to the highest vote getters without any representation for the
losers. Under winner-take-all, a slim majority (or plurality) can control all the votes leaving everyone else with no representation (in the
US most elections are held under the winner take all system).

Proportional representation. An election system whereby the los-
ing party (parties) are awarded representation in the government in
proportion to the percentage of the vote they receive (in the US, the
Democratic primary elections are run under proportional representation). <u>Proportional representation combined with a multi-party system represents the most democratic form of modern day government.</u>

Two round (second ballot) system. An election system where a
voter casts a single vote for his/her candidate, if no candidate receives
the required number of votes (usually a majority), then candidates
who reach a predetermined percentage of the vote (usually the top
two candidates) compete in a second (runoff) election.

One party system. In a one-party system only one party exists; form-
ing other parties is either forbidden or they are relegated into political
meaninglessness. A one-party system cannot be democratic except in
the very unlikely case that the party itself is run in a democratic manner. Cuba is ruled via a one-party system, the Communist Party.

CHAPTER **7**

Researching and Ranking Societies Rights and Freedoms

NOW THAT THE group of friends has determined what they are look-ing for in a Rawlsian society, they begin to research and rank the societies that they will be likely to be dropped into, would like to be dropped into, or have reservations about being dropped into.

The rights and freedoms the friends are looking for are found in a democracy with a constitution and bill of rights. The democracy can be direct, proportional, or presidential; multi-party, or two party… a multi-party democracy with proportional representation being the fairest. It can be run under either a parliamentary or presidential sys-tem, with elections culminating in results that distribute delegates fairly. Anarchism, totalitarianism, oligarchy, plutocracy, monarchy, and a one-party government disqualify countries from being consid-ered Rawlsian.

They will first award points for individual and political rights; next 5 points will be added or subtracted concerning a society's influence on world peace, and another 5 points concerning its environmental policies. A country will need to score at least 70 points to be consid-ered "Rawlsian."

After individual freedoms, political rights, world peace, and envi-ronmental policies are examined, societies will be ranked as to how well they score on the Rawlsian economic axiom: "inequalities are fine if when they are examined the greatest benefits from inequalities go to those who need them the most." (Rawls, 2001)

Political and Civil Rights

A country will be awarded 0-4 points for each of 10 political rights (40pts.) and 0-4 pts. for each of 15 civil rights indicators (60) pts. A score of 0 represents the smallest degree of freedom and 4 the greatest.

Political Rights. total 40pts.[1]

1. Is the head of state elected through free and fair elections?
2. Are the legislatures elected through free and fair elections?
3. Are the electoral laws and framework fair?
4. Do the people have rights to organize into political parties?
5 Is there opportunity for the opposition to increase its power through elections?
6. Are the people's choices free from domination by military, church, oligarchies, etc?
7. Do women and minorities have full political rights?
8. Do the elected heads of the government and legislature actually make the policies?
9. Is the government free from corruption?
10. Is the government accountable to the electorate between elections, and is it transparent?

Civil Rights. 60pts.

11. Are there free and independent media?
12. Is there freedom of religion, and from religion?
13. Is there academic freedom and is the system free of political indoctrination?
14. Is there open and free private discussion?

---

1   The institution that the friends utilized during their research is "Freedom House," a research institution devoted to examining freedom and democracy around the world (2018).

15. Is there freedom of assembly and freedom to demonstrate?
16. Is there freedom for non-governmental organizations?
17. Is there effective collective bargaining?
18. Is there an independent judiciary?
19. Does the rule of law prevail; are the police under civilian control?
20. Is there freedom from political terror, exile, torture, unjustified imprisonment?
21. Do laws, policies and practices guarantee equal treatment for all?
22. Do individuals enjoy the freedom to travel, and their choice of their residence, employment, and education?
23. Do individuals have the right to own property and establish businesses; and are businesses unduly influenced by the government?
24. Are there personal social freedoms such as gender choice, choice of marriage partners, and size of families?
25. Is there equality of opportunity and absence of economic exploitation?

For a country to be considered, that country must score at least 70 pts on criteria 1-25. Without satisfactory individual and political rights, a country will not be rated and cannot be considered fair and just. All societies then will be put to the economic tests.

Saudi Arabia. Saudi Arabia registered the lowest Freedom House 2016(FH) score of all countries studied (12pts), in addition the group deducted 3pts. since Saudi Arabia's actions and policies are considered detrimental to world peace and its proliferation of oil is a detriment to the environment.

Saudi Arabia is a true kingdom, not a constitutional monarchy. Its "constitution" is the Holy Book of Mohammed (the Koran) and the "Basic Law." The Basic law states the rights of the Monarch, and that the "constitution" is the Koran. The "Basic Law" severely limits political rights and Individual freedoms. The following are some of the specific reasons that Saudi Arabia was marked down by FH:

- No national elections: The ruling family is continually in power, subject to its own succession rules. Recently local elections have been enacted in which women can run for election and hold office in local juristicions but only one percent of the elected offices are held by women.
- No religious freedom: The Koran is the constitution...atheism may be punishable by death.
- Political parties are forbidden
- Political dissent is criminal; protests are forbidden
- The state controls all media
- The judiciary is not independent
- Those accused of crimes have very limited rights
- Freedom of movement is restricted
- Women are not at all treated equally...they were not even allowed to drive until 2018.

Saudi Arabia: 12-3= 9 pts

There is absolutely no chance that Saudi Arabia could be considered a Rawlsian society.

Sweden. Sweden received the highest FH score of the countries examined (100). But the group deducted 2pts because Sweden is a major arms dealer. The group also decided to add one point back since Sweden welcomes refugees more readily than most countries.

Sweden is a constitutional monarchy, its constitution restricts the power of the King to ceremonial affairs. The following are the reasons for Sweden's Freedom House rating:

- Sweden has a constitution
- Elections are: free, with a multiparty system, and proportional representation (the best form of democracy)
- Government corruption is minimal

- The media are independent
- Unions are protected
- There is extensive freedom of speech and press
- Political parties and protests are accepted as normal
- Religious freedom is guaranteed by the constitution
- There is an independent judiciary
- There is freedom of movement both within and outside the country.

Sweden: 100-2+1=99 pts

Sweden is a prime candidate for Rawlsian economics.

Cuba. Cuba is a one-party Communist state. It does not even pretend to be a democracy except at the local level. It received the second lowest FH score, behind Saudi Arabia. Interestingly, Cuba is considered a far-left government, while Saudi Arabia is far right... it seems that dictators rule at the extremes. The friends considered Cuba's environmental and military policies both neutral, but due to Cuba's extreme concern with world health, they added a point to its freedom house score. The following are some of the specific reasons for Cuba's low Freedom House rating.

- Cuba has a constitution, but it does not provide for democracy
- Cuba has a one-party system, which eliminates democracy unless the party is democratic, which the Communist party is not.
- Political organizing outside the Communist Party is illegal
- Freedom to associate in large groups is restricted
- Freedom of movement for its citizens is restricted both within the country and for overseas travel.
- The military controls business and politics
- The state controls all business transactions
- The media are controlled by the state
- Courts are not independent

Cuba: 15 (+1) =16 pts

Cuba does not qualify for Rawlsian Justice

China. China is also a one party Communist state. As such, it has very limited individual rights and political freedoms. China is the most populous country in the world, and because of its large population it wields a great impact on the world's economic, environmental, and military situations. China is a nuclear power and has a permanent seat on the UN Security Council. Its economics will be reviewed later, but its environmental and military positions are relevant to our political and individual ratings.

China is the world's largest polluter, its coal plants pour billions of tons or carbon into the atmosphere, and these plants are rapidly increasing. However, China is also at the forefront of switching to renewable fuels such as wind and solar. Overall the friends decided not to influence China's freedom score due to its environmental policies as they seem neutral.

Over its history China has had a negative effect on world peace and security. It has had major confrontations (although not all out wars) with the US and Russia that threaten the very existence of our planet. Although China has not been as warlike as the US and Russia, it has not contributed in major ways to international peace. The friends decided to deduct one point for its military policies.

The following are some of the specific reasons for China's Freedom House rating:

- The Communist party monopolizes all political power: there are no opposition parties.
- The only elections held are at the local level, and even at that level the party has an overwhelming influence on who the candidates are.
- Although the party is trying to control corruption, it is still a very major problem.
- There are severe restrictions on religion. All religious activities must be registered with the government, and many religious practices are barred.
- There are restrictions on personal movement, both within the country and internationally.

- Family size is restricted, and permission must be given by the government for couples to have children.
- All media are operated either by the party or by the state. Websites of liberal medias (New York Times, Wall Street Journal, Facebook, Twitter) are blocked. Reporters, both Chinese and international, are harassed.
- Academic freedom is restricted on political issues.
- Freedoms of assembly and association are severely limited.
- There is only one union allowed, and this union is governmentally controlled. Nevertheless, there were more than 1,000 strikes in 2015.
- Women are underrepresented in both the government and the Communist party.
- The judiciary is not independent; it is controlled by the Communist Party.

China: 15pts.

China cannot be considered a Rawlsian society.

India. India is the second most populated country in the world, but doesn't have quite the political, military, or economic influence as China. Much of India's history has been clouded by its "caste system." The caste system divides society into four basic groups, lowest of them being "untouchables," who have almost no rights. In recent years this system has been severely restricted, but it still shows its head in many customs and informal class relations.

The caste system divides society into different occupations and social groups according to birth. There are four basic castes ranging from the Brahmins (the priestly caste), to the Kshatriyas (the administrators and rulers), to the Vaishyas (merchants, tradesmen, and farmers), and those who were totally outside the system (the untouchables) with almost no rights or social status at all. There is minimal interaction between these groups, and their political, economic, and social situations are totally different. It is an unfair and cruel system.

The caste system in India has been functioning since ancient times, although in recent years it has not only been restricted, but by the government's use of affirmative action many of its previous wrongs are in the process of being corrected. However, because of affirmative action, the lower classes are often stigmatized.

India has a constitution, and is a nuclear power, however it does not have a permanent seat on the UN Security Council. India is the most populated country to have an established democratic government— a parliamentary government, with a multi-party system and proportional representation. The following are some of the specific reasons for India's Freedom House rating:

- India is a democracy with a constitution
- India's elections are free and fair, with women and minorities voting in large numbers.
- Freedom of religion is stated in India's constitution, but it is not always sufficiently guaranteed by law enforcement.
- There are some restrictions on freedom of association and movement.
- Academic freedom is generally enforced, with some exceptions.
- Corruption is problematic.
- Unions are permitted, but government can ban strikes in some instances.
- The judiciary is independent, but the criminal justice system doesn't always provide equal justice for all.
- There is discrimination against LBGTs
- Female rights: There is some female representation in government, but Muslim and Hindu practices discriminate against women. Rape is a serious problem in India. In general, female children are not as well cared for as their male counterparts: in many cases if a female fetus is known, it is aborted.
- Property rights are not enforced equally for all classes
- There are still remnants of the "caste system"

The friends decided to deduct 5 points from India's FH score because of the lingering remnants of the caste system.

India: 77 (– 5 pts) = 72

India may be considered for Rawlsian status.

France: France is a powerful western European country having played a major role in two World Wars. It is a nuclear power and holds a permanent seat on the UN Security Council. France is a representative multiparty, parliamentary democracy with a constitution, along with free and fair elections held by way of a two-round system. It is very influential in the European Union (a group of nation-states bound together in various economic, military, and political alliances). France is one of the major destinations for refugees from the middle-eastern wars and thus has a swelling Muslim population. Although French laws prohibit discrimination due to religion, many French nationalists have been harassing these immigrants.

The following are some of the reasons for France's high FH rating:

- France is a democracy and holds free and fair elections.
- Political parties are the basis of French politics.
- There are some problems with corruption.
- There is freedom of religion.
- There is a free press.
- There is academic freedom.
- There is usually freedom of assembly and association, but because of the numerous outbreaks of terrorism in recent time, these rights have occasionally been curtailed.
- Trade unions are strong.
- LBGT rights are protected.
- French citizens are free to travel within their own country and abroad.
- Gender equality is enforced in most cases. Women hold 27% of the elected offices in the General Assembly but are still under-represented and underpaid in the workforce.

France: 91pts.
France is a candidate for Rawlsian status.

Russia. Russia is what is left of the former Union of Soviet Socialist Republics (USSR). The USSR was created after Russia's loss to the Axis powers in World War I and the Communist Revolution, both occurring in 1917. The various Soviets (Georgia, Ukraine, Belarus...) were intended by Lenin to be states organized for the benefit of workers and peasants. Russia was itself a Soviet, comprising about 50% of the USSR's population. All Soviets were under the one-party rule of the Communist Party. When Lenin (the major force behind the Communist Party) died, he was succeeded by Joseph Stalin who became the party's (and the USSR's) head and soon evolved into an absolute dictator. Stalin permitted no dissent; purges occurred, and thousands were executed.

During World War II Russia fought along with the Allied Forces, and while it sustained more losses than any nation during the conflict, it emerged victorious...and eventually became a superpower along with the United States. After Stalin died in the early 1950's a variety of more tolerant leaders followed the same basic policies of a Communist state: central planning, communal farming, with a non-market economy...until Gorbachov, who experimented with more openness in government, some market-based economics, and a reduction in the arms race with the US. The Soviet people embraced these reforms, becoming more and more involved in free market trade, and international finance, until a severe recession occurred in the late 1980's. They then turned on Gorbachov, embraced his rival Boris Yeltsin, who eventually dissolved the USSR into 15 independent countries with Russia itself being the largest both in area and population. Yeltsin abruptly resigned in December 1999, and Vladimir Putin was "elected" president. This is the current political situation in Russia.

Russia's government is a semi- presidential system with multi-parties represented, although they must meet the approval of the Putin run United Russia Party. Russia is one of the most powerful countries in the world militarily, politically, and economically. It holds one of the five permanent seats on the UN Security Council and is a nuclear power. Russia has a low FH score, and although its shortcomings are similar to the US (unfair elections, lack of equality before the law, prominence of the military, police brutality) these shortcomings are much more pronounced in Russia.

Listed are some other reasons for Russia's low FH score:

- Russia has a constitution, but it is frequently ignored.
- Engineered "elections." Elections, and candidates, are manufactured by the Putin government.
- There is absence of public political debate, political protests are prosecuted, and assinations of political opponents occur.
- There is little transparency in government, most decisions are made behind closed doors.
- Corruption is pervasive.
- The government controls most of the mass media…"out of step" reporters are harassed. The government has the power to shut down websites.
- Freedom of religion, guaranteed in the constitution, is not strictly enforced.
- Education is influenced by political propaganda.
- The Prosecutor General can declare a foreign firm, or an NGO, undesirable and close their offices.
- Labor strikes are theoretically allowed, but their organizers and participants are frequently prosecuted.
- The judiciary is not independent, but under the control of the executive branch.
- Torture and deaths are common while prisoners are in custody.
- LGTBs are subjected to discrimination.
- A citizen's freedom of movement is restricted within and outside Russia. Citizens must carry passports while traveling within Russia.

- Women are under-represented in politics and government
Russia: 22pts.
Russia is not a candidate for Rawlsian status.

United States: Since the downfall of the Soviet Union the US is unquestionably the most powerful nation on earth both economically and militarily. Because of its tremendous influence in today's world, the friends decided that they needed to know the basic social structure of the US.

> *"We hold these truths to be self-evident, that all men are created equal, that they are endowed by their Creator with certain unalienable rights, that among these are life, liberty, and the pursuit of happiness."*
> *Pre-amble to The US Declaration of Independence*

The "pre-amble" sounds nice, but what does it mean?

First, it does not mean, nor was it originally intended to mean, that all humans are created equal. As we have amply illustrated, all men (all humans) are not created equal: we have different natural traits and abilities. In fact, a major subject of this book is what a government should do because of these inequalities. Possibly what the founders meant was that "all men are equal before the law." However, this does not stand up under closer scrutiny either, since male slaves had no rights whatsoever. What the "preamble means then is: all white male, property owners, over the age of twenty-one are to be treated equally before the law—eliminating about 80% of the population. *The founders never had any intention of treating all human beings equally, nor even of treating all males over twenty-one equally...only white, male, property owners over twenty-one years of age were to be treated equally.* The original US system of government was not based on equality; it was based on personal liberties (advantages) for, wealthy, propertied, white men.

But that was in the late 1700's... and for that period— a period of monarchs, lords, and aristocracy; it was a progressive position. Things have changed since then, making equality more inclusive in the US: slavery was abolished, the 19th Amendment gave women the right to vote, the voting age was lowered to eighteen (so that all those who fought in our wars were able to vote), and property restrictions were removed from voting requirements.

The US Constitution specifies a *democratic, representative government;* with a president, upper and lower legislative houses, and an independent judiciary. The presidential electoral process is an indirect winner-take-all system, in which citizens vote for electors who in turn vote for a candidate; but the electoral college system has resulted in three cases in the last five presidential elections in which the candidate with the most votes lost the election. The "first past the post" system of determining victors used in most US elections encourages the formation of only two major parties (proportional representation encourages third parties, coalitions, and more possibilities for change and cooperation).

Another major problem with US democracy is that because of the way the US upper house (Senate) is elected (each state being allowed two senators, no matter what its population); voters from unpopulated states wield power dramatically out of proportion to their population. The two Senators from Alaska (pop. 1,200,000) wield as much power as California's (pop. 37,000,000). The Senate is not a fairly represented body.

Due to its *winner take all two-party system* which limits change, choice, and third parties; the undemocratic make-up of the powerful senate; and the corrupting influence of money in elections; US democracy is not as fair as it could and should be, although it is called a democracy, it borders on being a plutocracy.

Enacted shortly after the constitution, the US Bill of Rights is an enumeration of rights granted US citizens; overturning these rights is possible, but extremely difficult requiring arduous amendment processes. The various rights and amendments are sometimes not enforced or enforced unequally... these usually relate to racial issues. However, for the most part, the civil rights guaranteed in the US Bill of Rights *have* been enforced and are part of the US basic social system.

Listed are some of the reasons for the United States' FH score: The US was marked up for...

- Freedom of speech, press, and association, although in recent years reporters have been pressured to reveal their sources limiting their ability to gather news because of the fear their sources have of being exposed.
- Equality for women
- There are laws to protect same sex marriages in many states.
- Unions' rights to organize are enforced (although this enforcement is on the decline)
- There is freedom of movement both within and outside of the country
- Citizens have freedom to demonstrate and protest government policies
- There is freedom of and from religion.
- There is academic freedom
- The judiciary is autonomous.

The US was marked down for...

- Flaws in the electoral system (mentioned above)
- The Supreme Court's decision in the Citizens United case compromises the electoral process.
- Racial discrimination
- The tendency of localities to use criminal fines for raising money, rather than as a punishment, leads to excessive and unfair fines for minor offenses, the burden of which systemically falls on the lower classes.
- Excessive force used by police, especially against minorities
- The US has the largest prison population in the world, which reflects poorly on the criminal justice system.
- A "for profit" prison system that encourages incarceration

so that the companies owning and running the prisons can profit.

- Racial profiling is used in arrest procedures, which leads to the disproportional incarceration of minorities
- The judicial process is extremely expensive.
- Because of its continuing wars, vast military industrial complex, and soft stance on environmental issues, the friends decided to deduct 10 pts from its FH score.

The United States: (90-10) = 80pts

The US can be considered for Rawlsian status.

CHAPTER 8

Economic Fairness:
The Difference Principle

REMEMBER THAT: *SOCIAL and economic inequalities*
are to be arranged so that inequalities are expected to
be to everyone's advantage, with the least advantaged
benefiting the most. The distribution of wealth and in-
come, and positions of authority are to be consistent
with the basic liberties and equality of opportunity.
JOHN RAWLS (2001)

TO COMPARE *ECONOMIC* systems and rank societies according to economic fairness the friends needed to know the following economic concepts:

Capitalism

Capitalism is the investment of capital (money) to make a profit; it assumes that if self-interest is allowed free reign, it will produce an economic system that benefits all society. In a capitalist economy, a market brings together willing buyers and sellers, and allows the "invisible hand" of the market to link buyers with sellers and determine prices. The capitalist attempts to make a profit in each transaction by selling his product for more than he produced (or bought) it for. The capitalist then re-invests this profit in new plant and equipment with a goal of making even more money on his/her next transaction.

Mercantilism

Mercantilism was the first form of capitalism. In mercantilism, there is little or no labor employed by the capitalist (aside from transportation); profit is made only on the resale of the goods. Buying maple syrup cheaply in Vermont where it is harvested and selling it at a higher price in New York City where it is scarce, is an example of mercantilism. This process is carried out in a "marketplace."

Marketplace

A general term referring to any exchange of goods for money or other goods be it an actual physical marketplace, business, or stock market (Fulcher, 2004).

Industrial capitalism

Industrial capitalism involves investing capital *to produce a product* that will be put up for sale in the market-place, hopefully at a cost less than its selling price. In industrial capitalism labor is involved; the cheaper a capitalist's labor costs are, the cheaper the product can be sold for and the more people will buy it.

The industrial capitalist searches the marketplace to find the cheapest labor in order to favorably compete with other producers. He/she treats human labor as if it were any other commodity. Ignoring the Bible's Golden Rule and Kant's imperative, "never treat human beings as a means only," the capitalist uses his laborers as a "means only" to make profits (Wood, 2002). The capitalist will substitute machines for labor whenever it is economically feasible to do so, reducing much of human labor to the unskilled and unsatisfying chore of tending to these machines; or casting them off into the "reserve army of the unemployed." The abundance of unskilled workers (the reserve army of the unemployed) push down the price of labor until it is at or below the sustenance level (Marx, 1848). *The industrial capitalist wants the masses to be both numerous and impoverished so that they will work for less;* in the process capitalists profit while the masses become poorer and poorer, due to sustenance (or even less than sustenance) wages. There arise ever increasing inequalities in income and wealth.

The successful industrial capitalist needs to produce a product for a lower cost than his/her competitor (but still at a profit) so that knowledgeable buyers will buy his/her product rather than a competitor's more expensive one. Due to economies of scale, the more units produced, the cheaper each unit costs. The companies that are able to produce on the largest scale are usually the ones that can produce and sell their product for the lowest price, driving out their competition, thereby creating a monopoly. The drive to manufacture "more for less" leads to overproduction, necessitating larger markets to absorb the excess product. This leads to colonialism and imperialism as the capitalists use their colonies as a dumping ground to absorb the excessive production; and as a source of cheap labor and materials.

Keeping the wheels of production turning also requires everspending consumers; necessitating the creation of non-essential demand by shrewd advertising and marketing techniques. (Who can say that the most modern garage door opener, most advanced cell phone, high definition TV, are necessary for an individual to survive; but these non-essential items are needed for capitalist businesses to grow, depleting our natural resources, while the world's poor starve).

To sum it up: the successful industrial capitalist employs cheap labor to do mindless work, ever expanding his/her production, thereby depleting our natural resources to create profits; and in the process, he/she creates economic inequalities both within a nation and between nations.

There are three basic contradictions in industrial capitalism: the capitalist doesn't pay his workers enough to buy the products they produce, the division of wealth between the capitalist and his laborers creates great inequalities, and the constant growth needed for capitalist expansion drains and pollutes the earth's natural resources. At some point, capitalism will have to regroup if it and the world are to survive.

Finance Capitalism

Finance capitalism is a successor to industrial capitalism. Finance capitalism was created by the need for greater capital sources (money for development) needed for capital intensive industries such as steel, railroads, mining, and oil.

In 16th century England laws were passed enabling the creation of corporations that could sell "stocks" to individuals or groups (investors) to raise money. These investors (financiers) bought a portion of the corporation (represented by stock shares) and were entitled to a share of the profits (dividends). They could sell their stock in the company: if the value of the company went up, so did their stock, enabling many capitalists to obtain profit without having any interest, except a monetary one, in the companies they invested in. Eventually buying and selling became the main reason for owning stock, leading to the emergence of stock markets where stocks are bought and sold, generally for short term profits. This, in turn, led to the continuous growth demanded by investors who wanted their stocks to increase in value so that they could sell them at a profit. The mindset of the investors forced companies to concentrate on short term profits so that the investors could make their profits quickly and reinvest. The short-term outlook combined with ever needed growth forced the companies to look askance at what they were doing to scarce resources and the environment.

A great advantage to an investor in stocks is the limited liability law; a law that proclaims an investor in stock can only be held liable for the value of his stock; i.e., if a company (such as British Petroleum) creates a tremendous liability (oil spill), its investors lose only to the extent that their stock loses its value. Limited liability makes it much easier for corporations to raise huge amounts of capital; but it also allows the companies to be much more reckless in their actions because of their limited liability. What would stockholders' reactions have been to the British Petroleum oil spill if investors were personally liable for the damage the company caused?

Stockholders, being owners, are thought to hold the ultimate power over corporate actions. They usually meet once a year, to elect a Board of Directors (BOD) to represent them; the BOD then hires a manager(s) to run the company. But as finance capitalism developed it became the corporate managers who wielded the power. There are three reasons for this; first is that in large corporations it is very difficult to own (or assemble) a controlling stock interest. The second reason is that most stockholders do not have the interest to be involved in the daily aspects of their company or of assembling and organizing groups of interested stockholders to influence corporate decisions; the third reason is that most corporate stocks are owned by large trust funds that are not in the business of running companies, but of buying and selling stocks. This leaves running the company to a class of corporate managers accountable usually only in theory to their stockholders. These managers are actually accountable to their boards of directors, but the board members are almost always corporate executives themselves and serve on many different and often interlocking boards making it very easy for them (board members and corporate managers) to form insider groups. As part of these "corporate insider" groups they can extract extremely high pay from their corporations because their cronies (board members and corporate managers who also have high salaries) are the board members they report to: the entire process being detrimental to their typical stockholders (those stockholders who are not corporate board members).

Globalization

Globalization to this date is the most advanced stage of capitalism. It is a modern economic system in which geographical distance and nationality have become almost irrelevant due to advances in transportation, communication, and the internet; resulting in enormously increased economic and political power for large transnational corporations and Wall Street bankers. The "electronic herd," that is the money managers of giant banks and financial institutions who follow prices and markets via the internet (Wilder on Wall Street), is a product of financial capitalism and globalization (Friedman, 2000). The "herd" can shift its investments by buying or selling stocks and bonds at a moment's notice, destroying the economy and currencies of entire countries overnight (Friedman, 2000). A race to the bottom occurs as competition and the electronic herd influence transnationals to move their factories (capital) from country to country, lowering wage scales and devastating local economies as they go until they eventually reach the absolute bottom of the global wage scale, destroying much of the world's economy and natural resources in the process.

Unions cannot prevent the race to the bottom since if they demand more money or benefits for their members, the transnationals will move their factories and jobs out of the union's sphere of influence. The various secretive "free trade alliances" such as North American Free Trade Alliance (NAFTA) and the proposed Trans-Pacific Partnership (TPP) promote this sort of behavior by reducing tariffs and other trade barriers. Unions advocate the repeal of these free trade laws.

In a globalized economy, the power of transnational companies often outweighs the power (political and economic) of all but the most powerful nations. More and more modern so-called democratic governments are "owned" by trans-national companies in that these companies "finance" the politicians that control governments. Many so-called democracies are run for the transnationals these politicians serve, rather than the "people" they are supposed to be representing.

Advocates of globalization, and its close companion free trade, preach that together they create jobs and provide cheaper products for the world's consumers; but the jobs they create are paid at poverty levels...the workers cannot afford to consume what they produce.

In the initial stages of relocating jobs to countries with lower wages and less regulation, workers in the poorer country flock from their sustenance farms or low-level jobs to the new and more lucrative (but still sustenance level) employment of the transnational. The trans-national makes a profit from these laborers; it then takes the profit out of the host country, not improving the host country's infrastructure or welfare to any significant degree, but increasing the wealth of the company, its home office executives, and local politicians. As time goes on the native workers try to obtain a decent wage (usually by some type of unionization), the transnational then leaves for a different country with yet lower wages and restrictions, leaving the local economy destroyed since their workers abandoned their farms and their former jobs have disappeared. As the transnational moves to another country, another race to the bottom begins.

Neo-liberalism and the Washington Consensus

What I have so far described is "free-market capitalism" enhanced by globalization. In free market capitalism, the freedom of the marketplace and maximization of profits are the ultimate freedoms, without concern for the human impacts of its policies. In the neo-liberal's mind, wages should be totally left to the discretion of the marketplace, trade barriers dismantled, capital restrictions removed, and corporate taxes reduced or eliminated. Free-market advocates believe that by pursuing this policy the world will become economically better off...so far this has failed to materialize. The misleading figures of rising national incomes occur because the overwhelming high incomes of the rich bring up the average, while the incomes of the poor stay the same or slightly rise in the short term but fall as the transnational moves on to another country. People that advocate pure free-market capitalism are called "neo-liberals." Governments that promote this system are said to be following the Washington consensus.

In the neo-liberal world, governments are an arm of business — representing business interests while ignoring the needs of the masses (in other words, Fascist).

The axioms of the Washington consensus and neo-liberals are:

- An unregulated free market (both domestic and international) will lead to economic growth. Government regulations (including rules protecting unions, people, and the environment) should be minimal.
- Corporate taxes should be minimal to promote corporate expansion.
- Free trade will increase the economic growth of the participating countries; therefore, tariffs and trade barriers are a detriment to international trade and prosperity.
- Increasing the GDP will reduce overall poverty even as it increases inequality…history says otherwise.

Pure unregulated capitalism and globalization as exemplified by neo-liberals and the Washington Consensus are not compatible with the justness and fairness of Rawlsian society.

State Capitalism

State capitalism is an economic system within the capitalist umbrella in which some of the means of production are organized and managed by the state or publicly listed companies in which the state has a controlling share. Profits extracted by these state-run companies are used for the benefit of government officials, the people, or reinvested in the government corporations (the US Postal Service is an example of state capitalism). The state competes with private companies in this type of economy.

The Welfare-State (Social Democracy) – A Capitalist Hybrid

At the present time no capitalistic states are "pure free-market neo-liberal" economies, they are hybrids with some welfare characteristics. Pure capitalism means no government regulation of business at all... even the most devout neo-liberal capitalist states (the US and Britain) feel a need to soften the effects of harsh unregulated free market activities such as monopolies, poor working conditions, starvation wages, and child labor.

The welfare state takes this softening idea further, enhancing the social safety net by establishing reasonable minimum wages, enacting progressive taxes, supporting union activities, and subsidizing food, shelter, and health care. A state that pursues these practices is labeled a "welfare-state" as it is actively looking out for the "welfare" of all its citizens. To pay for its social safety net, the welfare state promotes high progressive individual taxation and high corporate taxes.

The welfare state considers government as an enabler rather than a detractor: a place to turn to in times of trouble. The welfare state is usually the result of a strong union movement which sets the tone for its own welfare and that of the rest of the economy. For unions to be strong, the state supports them with strong labor laws, minimum wage rates, and tariffs.

In welfare states the government, unions, and business work together for the benefit of all. However, *the basis of the welfare state is profit-making capitalism, not socialism (see below); it is motivated by the market, individualism, and quick profits. There is always pressure to expand, and pressure on the earth's resources and environment; whereas socialism is not profit driven, has a planned economy, and is not necessarily threatening to the environment.* The welfare state is often referred to as a social democracy although it is not socialism since it is based on profits.

The welfare-state's characteristics— encompassing the redistribution of income (via progressive taxes) and the social safety net— generate Rawlsian results. In some instances, the welfare state nationalizes key businesses for the benefit of all its citizens, when this happens, since these nationalized businesses do not need to turn a profit... socialism begins.

The welfare state is compatible with Rawlsian theory, but since it is under the capitalist umbrella of compulsory growth, its tendencies are not compatible with environmental sustainability. These tendencies can, however, be regulated.

Advantages and Disadvantages of Capitalism

Throughout modern history capitalism has been the driving economic force in "western economies;" with the fall of the Soviet Union it emerged as the world's dominant economic form. There is no doubt that capitalism has contributed to most of our material advances in science, technology, and mass production. It has been dominant in bringing the world to its present state in which there is the capacity to produce enough goods and services to support the present population at a reasonable standard. For this capitalism should be applauded.

However, along with this material progress there are drawbacks: Capitalism promotes needless waste of our natural resources by the production of useless products needed to keep the process of production moving, while it ignores the pollution these processes generate; it encourages war as a general economic stimulus, promotes inequality rather than the equalities of social justice; and on an ethical plane, capitalism promotes the traits of greed and selfishness along with a disproportionate concern for income and wealth. Capitalism, without the softening of the welfare state, is "survival of the fittest."

Although pure capitalism is not compatible with the Rawlsian ethical system, or the ecosystems of the world, modified capitalism (capitalism modified by progressive taxation, unions, and strong regulations of the welfare state) can be part of a true Rawlsian system.

Karl Marx believed that capitalism is a stage that humanity will pass through on its path to a better society: socialism (Marx & Engels, 1848). Marx's thesis, however, is only one of many possibilities ... it is as likely that capitalism will use up and/or pollute our resources, irreversibly change our climate, and drive human beings as we know them into extinction before we move on to the next stage, whatever that stage may be. In the meantime, neo-liberal capitalism is molding negative character traits that are difficult to reverse. What is the answer...is there an answer?

Socialism: A Different Path

During the 1920s a new form of economy and government emerged from the devastation of WWI...Soviet Communism. Soviet Communism could have become a new golden age of socialism (equality); but in fact, it turned into a ruthless dictatorship commanded by Joseph Stalin. Russia, known during the times of Stalin as the Union of Soviet Socialist Republics (USSR), became a cruel but powerful force that western nations and its own people feared. Most westerners wrongly equated Soviet Communism with socialism; in the process, equating socialism with dictators, cruelty, and the total nationalization of production. The truth is that communism is but one form of socialism, and even communism does not necessitate dictatorial power and cruelty.

The US establishment demonized the USSR; and because the US propaganda equated Russian Communism with all socialism, it demonized socialism in all its forms. Sadly, this demonization remains a factor in US politics and policies today. Other countries increased welfare and thus have a comfortable social safety net, but due to the powerful minority that derives excessive profits from capitalism and their control of the US political system, the demonization of any form of socialism in the US continues.

Socialism

A broad definition of socialism, described by Eric Fromme, is: *a social system in which "the free development of each individual is the ruling principle, and where the wealth of the world is considered common property to be shared by all."* (Fromm, 1955)

Unfettered capitalism creates ever widening inequality and environmental destruction, it is not structured according to the Rawlsian rule that the greatest benefits of inequality should go to the ones most in need. Capitalism rewards the wealthy and powerful and capitalists promote the illusion that wealth "trickles down" from the rich to the poor; Socialism attempts to correct these faults by progressive taxation and regulations. Reduced inequality is a socialist's goal; capitalism, especially neo-liberal capitalism, increases inequalities.

Socialists believe that a democratically elected government should own much of the land and means of production. That same government should also decide what and how much is to be produced, as well as what resources are to be used to produce it. Socialists insist that decisions concerning the use of our finite resources are too important to be left to the invisible hand of the market, or the greed of corporate executives…a planned economy is essential.

The goal of socialism is societies in which citizens' basic needs are guaranteed and in which every individual is entitled to a *meaningful* job; is free to choose his/her personal goals without being subjected to the humiliations of poverty, hunger, excessive health expenditures, lack of housing, and meaningless work; an earth in which pollution is minimized and natural resources are not squandered; in other words…a sane society (Fromme, 1955). It is a world where there are minimal class differences, where the earth we live on and share with other creatures is kept in harmony and not allowed to deteriorate… where everything that matters is not determined by profit.

A "sane society" is one that does not depend on war, strip mining, clear-cutting, and pollution to keep functioning; a sane society is one that when a new machine to save human effort is created, it is not perceived by workers as a job loss, but as a labor saving device for all; a sane society does not have to create mind-numbing consumerism to keep industry's wheels turning while devastating the world's resources, nor does it ever use humans as means only, rather than ends in themselves, (Wood, 2002). A sane society does not encourage arms sales and wars in order promote a strong economy.

According to the socialist, the benefits of an economic system should be divided among all citizens as fairly as possible. Socialists stress cooperative traits and group solidarity rather than the competition and individuality of capitalism; socialists believe that cooperation is as basic a human trait as competitiveness.

What the world has now are not sane societies, but insane societies! That is not to say that socialism doesn't have its faults: lack of motivation to work hard because of a stifling tax structure being one of them. Capitalism with its incentives has brought us a long way in the realm of production but comes up short in its distribution methods, lack of concern for the environment, and encouragement of negative traits. Many feel that capitalism is a system that we must pass through to arrive at socialism.

Types of Socialism

There are numerous types of socialism; what they have in common is a drive toward eliminating the contradictions of capitalism:

Socialist hybrids. Socialist hybrids, in contrast to capitalist hybrids, operate under the umbrella of socialism, but still use the incentives of private enterprise to spur the economy. Coming from the overall socialist sector, socialist hybrids own or control essential utilities and major businesses, provide social necessities, promote equality, and control both the type and number of products produced, thereby eliminating some of the contradictions of capitalism. However, socialist economies do feel the need for incentives for innovation and production, and thus are reluctant to reject capitalism in all aspects of their economy. Even the Communist country of Cuba is now in the process of "privatizing" a portion of its economy to give its people more incentives for energetic work and innovation, while keeping its major industries under government control. The most well-known attempt at achieving a socialist hybrid was made by the Union of Soviet Socialist Republics (USSR) in the 1980s under Premier Gorbachov who attempted to combine Soviet Communism with western capitalism. This attempt failed because the Communist Party leaders became greedy under the influence of incentives, the individual soviets competed for market share, causing the USSR to break up and become individual capitalist countries.

Democratic Socialism. Democratic socialism is a political ideology that advocates political democracy alongside social ownership of the *major* means of production. Whereas social democrats seek to "humanize" capitalism through state intervention, *democratic socialists see capitalism as inherently incompatible with democratic values of liberty and equality* and believe that the negative issues inherent to capitalism can only be solved by superseding private ownership with some type of public ownership. Under democratic socialism most, but not all, of the means of production are owned or managed by the government. Although John Rawls would probably favor Social Democracy over Democratic Socialism, democratic socialism would be compatible with most of his concepts.

Market Socialism. Market socialism is similar to state capitalism, but operates within a socialist framework, i.e., a socialist government encourages its nationalized businesses to earn profits which are then turned over to the government to be used for the benefit of the people. It would be as if all businesses were run as the US Postal Service (by the government), these businesses then compete and turn their profits over to the government.

Utopian Socialism. Utopian socialism consists of small communities where all citizens live together, share common property, work together at shared tasks, and self-govern (the Israeli kibbutz). There is little private property in these communities, called *"communes,"* ... one's personal items are generally their only possessions. These societies have not worked out; the world is not ready for their unique conceptions of how life should be lived (extended families, communal living quarters, shared marriage partners, etc.).

communism "with a small c." Communism spelled with a lower case "c" refers to the theoretical concept of communism, not the specific form it takes in the governments and economies of the Soviet Union and Cuba. Communism is an extreme form of socialism, stressing a classless society and economic equality. In a Communist society, the state owns all land, means of production, and capital. The state also controls the distribution of goods and services following the maxim, "from each according to his abilities, to each according to his needs." Some, but not all, communists advocate violent revolution to achieve their goals (Marx, 1875).

Communism. Communism with a capital "C" refers to Soviet and Cuban Communism. In both cases it is a dictatorial system consisting of a highly centralized government that owns and regulates all production and distribution; the government controls what resources are used, how much of these resources, and for what purpose; this includes both human and natural resources. The Communist government's total control of production means that workers are forced to perform whatever job that the state requires and wherever their services are needed. This control severely restricts individual freedom and is reprehensible to most people. In other forms of socialism although the state may own the processes of production and decide what will be produced and in what quantities, the workers are free to decide their occupation and place of residence. In a democratic state, the state is supposed to serve the individual; whereas in a Communist state the state has priority over the individual. Therefore, in Communist theory, the Communist rulers are perfectly within their rights to force workers to relocate, change jobs, etc., if it benefits the state.

Marxist Communist theory (of which both the former Soviet Union and Cuba practice) states that there is a "vanguard" that knows the direction to take towards true communism more thoroughly than the public and that this vanguard (the leaders of the Communist Party) must govern until all the remnants of capitalism are gone (Marx & Engels, 1868). In fact, at least in the Soviet Union and Cuba, the vangard never relinquishes its power. Because of this policy, the Communist single party system became a non-democratic form of government, not typical of other socialist states (or communism) and incompatible with Rawlsian theory due to its policies concerning individual and political rights. It is a shame that when most people think of socialism, the first things that come to their minds are the cruelties of the single party system that both the USSR and Cuba used.

Anarchism. Anarchism is usually considered socialist, although of a different nature than most socialisms. Where most socialists consider government an agent of the people working for a better community, anarchists believe the reverse: anarchists believe that government is the agent of the more powerful classes of society and it (government) helps to keep these classes in power. Thus, where mainstream socialists believe that government should step in to help those in need, anarchists believe that by government's elimination equality will be enhanced. Anarchists have some of the same desires as neo-liberals— they both believe in a very limited role of government — but these desires stem from vastly different beliefs. Neoliberals want less government so that their corporations can run rampant over workers, while anarchists want less government because they feel the government is just an arm of these very same corporations.

Anarchism should not be considered Rawlsian, since Rawls believes that government should be encouraging equality and helping the needy.

National Socialism (Fascist-state socialism). National Socialism (Italy under Mussilini, Germany under Hitler) is not socialism at all; it is called socialism because many people believe that the only definition of socialism is the nationalization of business. Socialism is the stressing of equality, nationalizing some essential businesses is a part of the equalization process; in socialism "nationalization" is

<u>necessary for the benefit of the people,</u> not for the *benefit of corpora-
tions and the wealthy* businessmen. <u>*National Socialism "nationalization" is for the benefit of corporations*</u> and *wealthy* which increases
inequality. **National Socialism is not socialism nor is it compatible
with Rawlsian theory.**

Conclusions. Socialism does not have all the answers, but it does
have many of the right goals, and they are not only economic goals.
The socialist goals of equality and co-operation are beneficial for
the community and help every individual in it to realize their potential as human beings. In the economic sphere, the socialist is ready
"to grab the bull by its horns," not relying on the "invisible hand"
of the market, but the "visible hand" of government to decide what
needs to be produced and how it will be produced and distributed
fairly in a sustainable manner.

Socialism's Advantages and Disadvantages

The advantages of socialism lie in the goals it sets for itself and
the human traits it promotes, especially those of equality and free
development of the total individual. When its goals can be made
part of a society's basic social structure, that society will be the better for it. However, the goals of socialism are too idealistic for present day society brainwashed with capitalism and are unlikely to be
attained in the foreseeable future, if ever.

Socialism, as with capitalism, has its drawbacks. The most fundamental drawbacks of socialism are:

- The total commitment of communism to equality is too
idealistic: "from each according to his ability, to each according to his needs" is not a workable arrangement: The
incentives to invent and produce new and efficient methods
and products are likely to be reduced if material benefits
are not awarded to those who do the inventing and producing; the lack of personal incentives for workers can increase
laziness.

- The socialist belief in the goodness of human beings is just as naive as the capitalist belief that greed and selfishness are beneficial human qualities. Some humans are good, others not so good; some greedy, some altruistic; some lazy, and some productive.

- Nationalization of numerous vital industries creates a huge bureaucracy which will likely treat individuals with much of the coldness and lack of concern that are chatacteristic of the capitalist.

- The socialist stress on cooperation and group solidarity conflicts with the benefits derived from competition and individual effort.

The basic structure of socialism is compatible with Rawlsian theory (except for the dictatorial traits of Communism). Rawls, however, allows for more exceptions to equality in his difference principle than do socialist societies.

Cooperatives

One of the most interesting economic forms are cooperatives. They cannot be categorized as either socialist or capitalist, which is one reason why their potential is so great. If a key word for capitalism is competition; then a key word for cooperatives is, naturally, cooperation. There are two major forms of cooperatives: *economic co-operatives and co-operative communities.* Cooperative communities are self-contained entities in which social cooperation, equality, democratic governing procedures, shared community housing, and a communal work ethic are the way of life (the Utopian socialist communities previously described)...there is little in the way of co-operative communal movements throughout the world at the present time.

Current US law defines an *economic* cooperative as "a corporation or association organized for the purpose of rendering economic services without gain to itself, to shareholders, or members who own and control it," (Williams, 2007). *"This makes it (the co-operative) a small unit of socialism within a capitalist world,"* (Scott, 2008). An example of a co-operative is a group of dairy farmers pooling their resources to hire a trailer to take their milk to market... saving them all the expense of buying their own vehicles. Economic cooperatives exist in both developed and developing countries, offering a more advantageous system for competing on the open market. It is a way for small businesses and individuals to compete with transnational companies, while indoctrinating themselves with the benefits that cooperation offers (Williams, 2007). Capitalism is currently the world's foremost economic system, and co-operatives are a unique way of introducing efficient production, distribution, and financial mechanisms within it by means of cooperation rather than competition.

Economic co-operatives take various forms: producer co-ops, value-added co-ops, distribution co-ops, service co-ops, retail co-ops, artisan co-ops, housing co-ops, and financial co-ops. Although co-ops differ in their functions, they all have commitments to collective ownership and democratic decision making (Williams, 2007). The greatest contribution of economic cooperatives, however, may not lie in their economic functions, which are very significant; but in their contribution to a different type of social thinking, one in which the social justice theories developed by John Rawls and Wilder's group are put into actual practice—a way for the self-centered, capitalist mindset to be modified from "the bottom up."

There are no Rawlsian objections to cooperatives, but there is a limitation: their operation as an island within the capitalist system limits their ability to control major world-wide problems such as pollution and the depletion of natural resources. The overall goals of co-operatives are to foster cooperative traits to make life more meaningful and productive, and to reduce costs to promote the business efficiency of its members so that they can *compete* better in their market. Co-ops as a socialist island in a capitalist system can't control the environmental devastation inherent in capitalism, but they can foster a basic social awareness of co-operation. Some present-day co-operatives are REI, the Green Bay Packers, the Kerala province in India and the Basque province in Spain. During the communist reign of the Soviet Union there were many cooperatives, especially in the field of agriculture, but they were forceful, state run, and dictatorial.

Democratically run co-operatives are key to favorably changing the basic social structure of society and totally consistent with Rawls' theory.

BOOK III

CHAPTER 9

Comparative Economic Systems

IN THIS PHASE of their investigation, the souls focus on the economic systems of the countries that they have politically evaluated.

- Are social and economic policies arranged so that inequalities are to be to everyone's advantage, with the least advantaged benefiting the most?
- What is the actual distribution of wealth and income?

Terms

They need to be familiar with the following terms to complete their surveys:

Average, Mean, and Median

Average and mean are the same. They are computed by adding entries and then dividing by the number of entries. The median is the middle value of a set when the set is ordered by rank. Example: (6, 9, 12, 18, 24, 85, 615). The median number in this case is 18, while the average is 109.85. As you can see, these numbers are quite different. If a few super-wealthy people move into a state, the wealth figure will be distorted if an "average" number is used. In this situation, the preferred method would be a median number. *When accessing income, wealth, and population figures, one should be aware of this.*

Gini Coefficient

The Gini coefficient measures the income (and/or wealth) inequality of a group. A Gini coefficient of 1 means that a group is totally unequal (e.g., a large group of people in which one person obtains all the income…the landlord in a feudal system). A Gini coefficient of "0" indicates the reverse, a society in which all are granted equal income (utopian communism). The Gini Coefficient should be measured both before and after taxes. A country may allow large income inequalities before taxes (producing a larger before tax Gini Coefficient), only to level out after-tax income by progressive taxation. The more important number is, obviously, the after-tax Gini. A problem using the Gini Coefficient is that figures are not available for most undeveloped and developing countries.

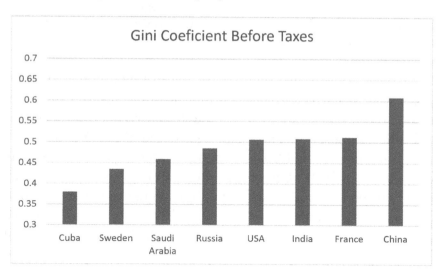

As can be seen from the above graph, before taxes are taken into consideration Cuba has the most economically equal society, while China has the greatest gap between its rich and poor citizens. However, once taxes are figured into the equation, things change:

93

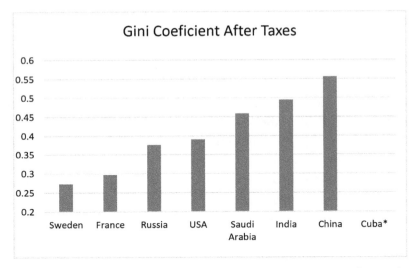

Gini Coeficient After Taxes

*There is no information available on Cuba's after-tax Gini Coefficient, but it does have a progressive income tax, and its before tax Gini was very low, so it will have a very low after tax Gini.

Sweden, out of the countries we are examining, has the most equal after tax economy, with China again being the most un-equal. We can also see from the graph that France's position has radically changed when taxes are considered. France's progressive tax policy has leveled out an unequal wage structure. From the graph below, which subtracts the after-tax Gini from the before tax Gini, we see that both France and Sweden use taxation to equal-ize income; Cuba also does so, but there are no figures available to compare it with other countries; Saudi Arabia has no personal income tax.

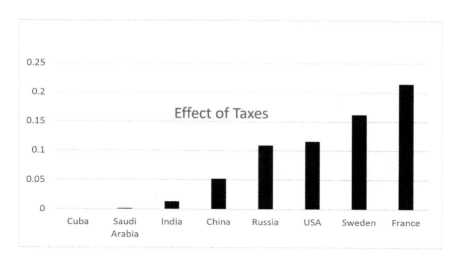

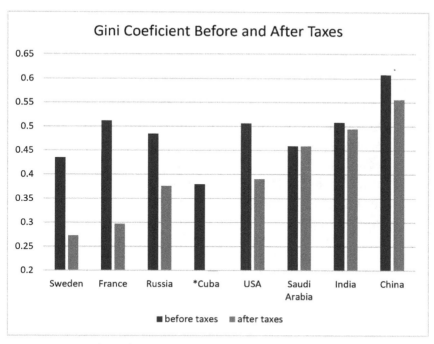

(source: Wikipedia)

Gatsby Coefficient

The Gatsby coefficient plots the likelihood that offspring will inherit their parents' relative income position. As with the Gini coefficient, 1 represents the total likelihood that children will inherit their parents' relative income position, while "0" indicates that there is no correlation between the income of parents and the income of their offspring. The major problem with using the Gatsby Coefficient is that figures are not available for most countries.

Among the countries studied by the friends, the ones that a Gatsby Coefficient is available for are: US .48, France .4, and Sweden .28...indicating that, at least among these countries, it is easiest to advance one's social/economic status in Sweden and toughest in the US. *Natural attributes and drop in society are essential in the US: not as much in Sweden.*

Conclusions:

From the graphs they studied, all the friends but one preferred Sweden or France as their country of choice (more actually preferred Sweden due to its lower Gatsby coefficient); the only holdout was Vic, who, because of ❓strong work ethic and confidence in ❓abilities, chose the United States, which has a limited democracy and low social safety net. The others did not want to trade in the security of the social safety net for the rather unlikely chance of being dropped into an advantageous society with above average personal traits...Vic must be feeling mighty lucky.

CHAPTER 10

The Left and the Right Revisited

THE LEFT AND the Right. In politics and economics there is constant talk of "the left," and "the right." According to popular history the terms left and right derived from the seating arrangements of the legislature during the early phase of the French Revolution, taken from the view of the speaker. Over the years specifics have changed slightly, but the individuals on the speaker's left generally desire equality, large government, and extensive democracy; while those on the right are tolerant of greater inequality, want limited government, and restrictive democracy, plutocracy, or authoritarianism.

Figure 1

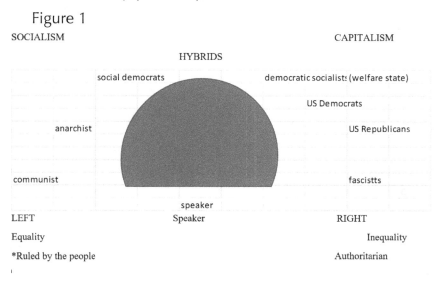

SOCIALISM   CAPITALISM

                              HYBRIDS

social democrats   democratic socialists (welfare state)

                                            US Democrats

anarchist   US Republicans

communist   fascistts

                        speaker

LEFT   Speaker   RIGHT

Equality   Inequality

*Ruled by the people   Authoritarian

*In theory communism develops into a classless system in which formal government "withers away" and the workers rule themselves. In practice this is generally not true, the very extreme left has existentially, although not theoretically, been authoritarian.

The above illustration encompasses the whole political/economic spectrum.

In the US pro-capitalist world of 2018, the actual political chart looks like this:

Figure 2

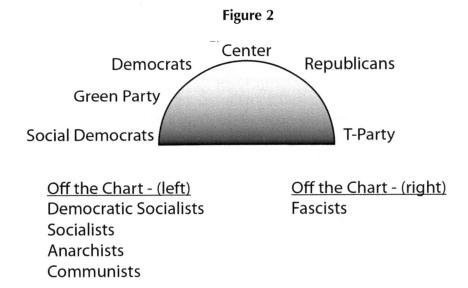

Off the Chart - (left)
Democratic Socialists
Socialists
Anarchists
Communists

Off the Chart - (right)
Fascists

Most citizens of the US mistakenly equate Social Democrats (the welfare state) with the far left...some even going as far as referring to Social Democrats as Communists. **It is important to note that the US graph (figure 2) only comprises the right half of the political/economic graph illustrated in Figure 1.** The political center in the US graph (figure 2) is between the US Democrats and the US Republicans. This is a distorted way of viewing politics and economics and helps us to understand why there is so much fear of socialism in the US. The political center of the graph should be between the Social Democrats (slightly to the right), and the Democratic Socialists (slightly to the left).

Sweden and France are both politically and economically social democratic states and are thus under the capitalist, rather than the socialist, umbrella, and succumb to a fundamental capitalist law — the constant need to expand, which results in overstressing the earth's resources and waste. Sweden and France are heavily involved in arms trading, an extremely wasteful and destructive way to generate business: useful for creating profits and expansion, but wasting resources, both human and material. If they were democratic socialist, they would not need to show growth and profit by continuously expending their resources and promoting the killing and destruction of war. The government could plan the economy so that it doesn't need the constant expansion required by capitalism, but still allows an amount of free enterprise — -especially in the service, tourism, and retail sectors.

Does a solution need to be either/or— socialism or capitalism— on either the far left or far right of the graph? Justice and fairness lie in the center of the first graph, not a graph skewed to the right (as is the US graph). It is obvious to the friends (even Vic) that the solution is not either capitalism or socialism but using the best aspects of each to promote justice and fairness: which is the center of the first graph... between the social democrats and the democratic socialists.

Are there any societies economically and politically like Sweden and France that are less involved in militaristic endeavors and the wasting of natural resources? The friends didn't know the answer to this question but vowed to research it when they returned from their upcoming lives. On their return the friends will discover that there are at least two countries that fulfill these requirements, but they are small and have abundant renewable resources...Iceland and New Zealand. For larger countries to achieve this status, they will have to inject some democratic socialism into their economic system (meaning more regulation) and the nationalization of some key industries. The world is not ready for these steps yet, but it will have to take them if we are to survive as a species.

References – APA format

Carter, F. (1976). *The education of little tree*. Albuquerque, NM: University of New Mexico Press.

Crisp, R. (1998). *J. S. Mill*. Oxford, UK: Oxford University Press.

Freedom House (2018). www.freedomhouse.org

Friedman, T. (2000). *The Lexus and the olive tree*. NY: Anchor Books.

Fromm, E. (1955). *The sane society*. NY: Henry Holt and Company

Global Issues, Poverty Facts and Stats. www.globalissues.org

Marx, K. (1990). *Capital*. NY: Penguin Classics.

Marx, K. & Engels, F. (1992). *The communist manifesto*. NY: Oxford University Press.

Marx, K. (1875). *The essential writings of Karl Marx*. St. Petersberg, FL: Red and Black Publishing.

Rawls, J. (2001). *Justice as fairness*. Cambridge, MA: Harvard University Press.

Scott, H. (2008). *The essential Rosa Luxemburg*. Chicago, IL: Haymarket Books.

Smith, A. (2008). *An inquiry into the nature and causes of the wealth of nations*. Hamburg, GR: Management Laboratory Press.

Steinbeck, J. (1945). *Cannery row*. Garden City, NY: Sun Dial Press.

Sunstein, C. (2004). *The second bill of rights*. NY: Basic Books

Williams, R. (2007). *The cooperative movement.* Burlington, VT: Ashgate Publishing Company.

Wikipedia. *List of countries by income equality.*

Wikipedia. *Gatsby curve.*

Wood, W. (2002). *Groundwork for the metaphysics of morals.* New Haven, CN: Yale University Press.

World Income Distribution. www.imagesforworldincomedistribution.

CPSIA information can be obtained
at www.ICGtesting.com
Printed in the USA
FSHW011606220419
57441FS

9 781478 767190